The Work Sampling System®

Omnibus Guidelines
Kindergarten through Fifth Grade

The Work Sampling System is a performance assessment that provides an alternative to group-administered, norm-referenced achievement tests in preschool through fifth grade. Its purpose is to document and assess children's skills, knowledge, behavior, and accomplishments across a wide variety of curriculum areas on multiple occasions.

The Work Sampling System consists of three complementary elements:

1) Developmental Guidelines and Checklists,
2) Portfolios of children's work, and
3) Summary Reports.

Assessments based on the Work Sampling approach take place three times a year. They are designed to reflect classroom goals and objectives and to help teachers keep track of children's continuous progress by placing their work within a broad, developmental perspective. Through its focus on documenting individual performance of classroom-based tasks, Work Sampling enhances student motivation, assists teachers in instructional decision-making, and serves as an effective means for reporting children's progress to families, professional educators, and the community.

Omnibus Guidelines

Kindergarten through Fifth Grade

3rd Edition

Judy R. Jablon
Lauren A. Ashley
Dorothea B. Marsden
Samuel J. Meisels
Margo L. Dichtelmiller

The Work Sampling System®

REBUS PLANNING ASSOCIATES, INC.
ANN ARBOR, MICHIGAN

For more information about
The Work Sampling System, write to:
Rebus Planning Associates, Inc.
1103 South University Avenue
Ann Arbor, Michigan 48104

Preparation of this document was supported in part by a grant from the John D. and Catherine T. MacArthur Foundation. The opinions expressed are solely those of the authors.

DESIGNED AND PRODUCED BY MODE DESIGN.

Printed in the United States of America.

96 95   10 9 8 7 6 5 4 3

Part No. 31112 (10/94)
ISBN 1-57212-101-7

Introduction · **vii**

I Personal and Social Development · · · · · **1**
A Self concept · 2
B Self control ·6
C Approach to learning · · · · · · · · · · · 14
D Interaction with others · · · · · · · · · · 22
E Conflict resolution · · · · · · · · · · · · · 32

II Language and Literacy · · · · · · · · · · · · **39**
A Listening · 40
B Speaking · 44
C Literature and reading · · · · · · · · · · · 48
D Writing · 60
E Spelling · 76

III Mathematical Thinking · · · · · · · · · · · · **81**
A Approach to mathematical thinking · · · · · · 82
B Patterns and relationships · · · · · · · · · · · · 86
C Number concept and operations · · · · · · · · 92
D Geometry and spatial relations · · · · · · · · 104
E Measurement · · · · · · · · · · · · · · · · · · 110
F Probability and statistics · · · · · · · · · · · 118

IV Scientific Thinking · · · · · · · · · · · · · · **125**
A Observing and investigating · · · · · · · · · · 126
B Questioning and predicting · · · · · · · · · · 134
C Explaining and forming conclusions · · · · · 138

V Social Studies · · · · · · · · · · · · · · · · · · **145**
A Human similarities and differences · · · · · · 146
B Human interdependence · · · · · · · · · · · · 150
C Rights and responsibilities · · · · · · · · · · · 158
D People and where they live · · · · · · · · · · 164
E People and the past · · · · · · · · · · · · · · · 170

VI The Arts · **173**
A Expression and representation · · · · · · · · · 174
B Artistic appreciation · · · · · · · · · · · · · · · 180

VII Physical Development · · · · · · · · · · · · **185**
A Gross motor development · · · · · · · · · · · 186
B Fine motor development · · · · · · · · · · · · 190
C Personal health and safety · · · · · · · · · · · 196

Resources · **203**

Acknowledgements · · · · · · · · · · · · · · **209**

Introduction

This volume presents the compilation of the Work Sampling System Developmental Guidelines for kindergarten through fifth grade. A companion volume presents the Guidelines for preschool through third grade. The Omnibus Guidelines provides the opportunity to view six years in the Work Sampling System's developmental continuum.

The Work Sampling System's Developmental Guidelines are designed to enhance the process of observation and to ensure the reliability and consistency of teachers' observations. The Guidelines incorporate information from a wide array of resources, including local, state, and national standards for curriculum development. These resources are listed beginning on page 203.

How to read the Guidelines. The Guidelines present each specific skill, behavior, or accomplishment in the form of a one-sentence *performance indicator.* Each indicator is followed by a *rationale* and several specific *examples.* The rationale provides a context that explains the meaning and importance of the indicator and briefly outlines reasonable expectations for children of different ages. The examples show several ways children might demonstrate the skill, knowledge, or accomplishment represented by the indicator. Since different teachers may interpret the same indicator in different ways, the Guidelines promote consistency of interpretation and evaluation across children, teachers, and schools.

Although the examples provided for each indicator suggest a variety of ways that children show their skills and knowledge, they do not exhaust all the ways children demonstrate what they know and can do. The students in any particular classroom may show their knowledge in other ways, reflecting their unique backgrounds, interests, and classroom opportunities. We expect that our examples will serve as a catalyst to help teachers think of the range of situations in which children demonstrate specific skills and knowledge, and to understand and evaluate their students' performance within the context

Introduction continued

of their classrooms. Other examples that are more consistent with an individual teacher's curriculum approach can be added.

In the Guidelines, we have attempted to provide illustrations that are relevant to teachers who work with diverse groups of children. Examples that relate specifically to the development of children with special needs are included to suggest how teachers might assess children with disabilities who are included in regular classrooms. Rather than providing examples related to specific cultural or linguistic groups, we have tried to use inclusive or general language to accommodate children from various cultural, linguistic, economic, and social backgrounds.

The Work Sampling System is a dynamic approach to assessment. It is intended both to inform and reflect best practice. We encourage teachers to use it as a framework for meeting and assessing the needs of all students.

About the Omnibus Guidelines format. Each set of facing pages presents a single performance indicator (along with its rationale and examples) as it progresses through six years. This format allows the examination of the growth and development of a wide range of skills, abilities, and behaviors of children across that six year span.

Each grade level's Guidelines is also published separately in an edition designed to facilitate classroom use. Thus this Omnibus Guidelines is a compilation of six documents, presented in parallel format. Most indicators appear in all six grade levels; however, for those that do not, or those that are included in other indicators, the sentence "No equivalent performance indicator at this level" appears in their place. Furthermore, although indicator numbering is sequential within a single grade, in this edition the same indicator may have different numbering in different grades. Referring to a single grade-level indicator by its grade (e.g., Kindergarten), domain (e.g., II. Language and Literacy), functional component (e.g., B. Speaking), and indicator number (e.g., 2) will result in an unambiguous reference (K-II-A-2) that is consistent throughout all the materials in the Work Sampling System.

Our values. Every assessment is guided by a set of values about learning and instruction, and how children should be treated in order to enhance their growth and development. The values of the Work Sampling System are based on the attributes of well-functioning children, as suggested by the work of June Patterson and others. These attributes are that all children can:

- Learn to trust themselves and others;

- Learn self discipline;

- Gain an awareness of others and the ability to feel for and with them;

- Be spontaneous when expressing feelings;

- Become self-reliant and self-starting;

- Become increasingly responsible for their own behavior and safety;

- Develop a sense of humor;

- Form creative ideas;

- Extend basic moving, manipulating, and communication skills;

- Listen with heightened and prolonged attentiveness;

- Acquire factual information, and develop the capacity to conceptualize and represent ideas;

- Have a variety of interests and resources;

- Find pleasure in the process as well as in the product; and

- Show the desire to try, the courage to fail, and the persistence to continue their effort.

We hope that these values will imbue teachers' work with greater professional satisfaction and enhanced learning opportunities for children.

I

Personal and Social Development

This domain has a dual focus. First, it refers to children's feelings about themselves. The teacher can learn about these feelings by observing children, listening to their comments, and hearing families talk about their children. Included in this focus are indicators that refer to children's views of themselves as learners, and their sense of responsibility to themselves and others. The second focus concerns their social development, including children's interactions with peers, and adults. Particularly important are the skills children show they are acquiring while making friends, solving conflicts, and functioning effectively in groups.

I Personal and Social Development

A Self concept

Kindergarten	First Grade	Second Grade
1 Shows comfort and confidence with self.	**1 Shows comfort and confidence with self.**	**1 Shows comfort and confidence with self.**

Kindergarten

1 Shows comfort and confidence with self.

Self-awareness and positive self image grow through interactions with others and through experiences of being effective. Five year olds display a positive sense of self by:

• entering established groups confident they will be accepted;

• suggesting roles for themselves in dramatic play or blocks;

• coping well with personal awkwardness or mistakes when trying new tasks;

• entering the classroom in the morning with the assurance they are expected and accepted;

• enjoying the creative process and expecting that their accomplishments will be appreciated by others;

• explaining their disabilities and coping strategies to able-bodied children.

First Grade

1 Shows comfort and confidence with self.

Six year olds are still eager to please adults and often depend on praise to feel competent. Acquiring self-awareness and confidence is a gradual process that occurs through children's interactions with others and repeated experiences of being effective. Examples of how six year olds demonstrate comfort and confidence include:

• easily choosing a work or play partner (for example, during a choice time, or outdoor play);

• working or playing alone or with a friend without needing frequent adult support or approval;

• explaining their disability to a new child in the classroom;

• coping reasonably well when things don't work out exactly as planned (for example, trying to draw a picture of someone and not having it look exactly right).

Second Grade

1 Shows comfort and confidence with self.

Seven year olds, frequently more self-conscious than five and six year olds, can be somewhat self-critical. Acquiring self-awareness and confidence is a gradual process that occurs through children's interactions with others and repeated experiences of being effective. Examples of how seven year olds demonstrate confidence include:

• choosing a work or play partner based on friendships or shared interests (for example, someone who likes to play chess or is interested in making models);

• saying a friend's painting is great, but then not putting down their own work;

• coping reasonably well with not winning a game or not being partnered with a friend;

• asking for needed assistance in appropriate ways.

Third Grade

1 **Shows comfort and confidence with self.**

By eight years of age, many children are deeply invested in peer opinions and will do much self-comparison. Independence and self-confidence are often difficult to see because third graders are motivated to be like their peers. Examples of how an eight year old demonstrates comfort and confidence include:

• choosing work or play partners based on shared interests, such as writing with someone who also likes adventure stories;

• developing strategies for coping with difficult feelings (for example, seeking an alternate playmate when rejected by the first choice of play partner, knowing to take a break when frustrated by things not going right, or being able to laugh off mistakes);

• evaluating their own work and discussing it critically;

• recognizing that one's value is not diminished when others are also valued (such as recognizing that someone else's strategy for solving a math problem is more efficient than one's own).

Fourth Grade

1 **Shows comfort and confidence with self.**

Fourth graders work and play with others effectively when they feel confident about themselves emotionally and physically. By nine years of age, children are beginning to appreciate their own self-worth. They strongly identify with members of their own sex and show growing assertiveness in defending their own rights. Examples of how nine year olds demonstrate comfort and confidence in self include:

• showing willingness to perform a variety of roles in cooperative group work (e.g., note taker, facilitator, presenter);

• presenting to an audience with confidence;

• participating in activities that require physical actions (athletics, dancing, pantomime);

• evaluating their own work and recognizing personal strengths;

• sharing projects from home that were done independently of school.

Fifth Grade

1 **Shows comfort and confidence with self.**

For fifth graders, confidence is often tied to peer acceptance. Their tendency to worry about how others perceive them, friendships, and personal competencies can sometimes obscure their otherwise positive feelings about themselves. They are beginning to evaluate peers on physical appearance and they wonder how others are judging them. Examples of how fifth graders demonstrate comfort and confidence include:

• feeling good about completed work and wanting to share it with others (for example, artwork, writing, a new song learned on a musical instrument);

• being supportive of others in difficult situations;

• taking the less-interesting role in a play because no one else is willing to do it;

• working and playing with others in ways that recognize personal boundaries;

• accepting leadership responsibility in a group.

I Personal and Social Development

A Self concept continued

Kindergarten	First Grade	Second Grade

Kindergarten

2 Shows initiative and self-direction in actions.

Independence in thinking and action enables children to be creative and take responsibility for their lives. Children often need help from adults as they begin to expand their independence. Some examples of independence are:

• originating projects and working on them without extensive direction from the teacher;

• finding materials for projects, such as scissors and tape to build a house out of a cardboard box;

• finding their outdoor clothes and dressing without extensive teacher supervision;

• assuming classroom chores without being asked (for example, sweeping sand from the floor, watering the plants, helping to clean up spilled juice);

• knowing how and where to stack blocks at clean-up time.

First Grade

2 Shows initiative and self-direction in actions.

Six year olds want to try new things, but often overestimate their capabilities. Examples of how they demonstrate initiative and self-direction include:

• thinking up a project and working on it without extensive teacher direction;

• helping with extra clean-up responsibilities in the classroom;

• transporting personal belongings to and from school (for example, homework, backpack, notes to family members);

• volunteering help to a peer having difficulty coming up with a story idea;

• explaining to someone the kind of help they need to play a game (for example, "Put the game on the tray of my wheelchair so I can reach it.").

Second Grade

2 Shows initiative and self-direction in actions.

Many seven year olds are both eager to use newly acquired skills and fearful of not doing things exactly right. They demonstrate initiative and self-direction by:

• willingly and independently taking on extra responsibilities in the classroom (for example, an extra clean-up task, setting up a display, or caring for the plants);

• making independent decisions despite peer pressure to do something else, such as deciding to finish a computer project instead of going to recess;

• assuming responsibility for personal needs (for example, readily finding one's journal or reading book, bringing or wearing sneakers on gym days);

• appropriately declining help that is offered but not needed.

Third Grade

2 Shows initiative and self-direction in actions.

By eight years of age, children are developing preferences and interests that may be more aligned with those of their peers than with those of adults. They demonstrate initiative and self-direction by:

• completing homework and bringing it to school on time;

• making independent decisions despite peer pressure to do something else (such as deciding to draw a mural even though close friends will be playing a board game);

• initiating independent projects (for example, learning how to play the recorder, writing a play based on a favorite book);

• helping a group organize a project without being bossy;

• suggesting an adaptation that will allow them to participate more fully in a classroom activity.

Fourth Grade

2 Shows initiative and self-direction in actions.

By nine years of age, students begin to act with independence in response to their own opinions and desires. They seek new experiences and will more readily muster courage to attempt unfamiliar challenges. They demonstrate initiative and self-direction by:

• choosing a variety of activities within a subject area instead of always doing what has been successful (e.g., selecting different types of literature projects, creating different models, choosing different software programs);

• tackling difficult tasks and maintaining a sense of humor during trial and error;

• playing the role of an opposite sex character in a play because of interest in the part despite comments from peers;

• selecting a partner based on shared interests despite pressure from peers to act otherwise.

Fifth Grade

2 Shows initiative and self-direction in actions.

Fifth grade students often have very clear ideas and opinions about what they want to do and how they want to do it, and this can lead them to work successfully on their own. They demonstrate initiative and self direction by:

• making a plan for a long-term project and seeing it through from beginning to end;

• organizing a group game on the playground and working to make the game successful for all;

• choosing a variety of activities within a subject area instead of always doing what has been successful (trying different ways of taking notes, selecting different types of literature projects, writing stories in different genres or tenses);

• selecting project partners based on shared interests despite pressure from peers to select someone else.

I Personal and Social Development

B Self control

Kindergarten

1 Follows classroom rules and routines.

Children who are successful within a group know and accept the rules established for that particular group. Five year olds are learning this skill and can be quite dogmatic with their peers, insisting on adherence to the rules. They are comfortable when they know the routines and can plan their activities around the daily schedule. Ways that children show this ability are:

• knowing that only three people can be at the work bench at one time and choosing another activity until space is available;

• recognizing that because it is almost time for snack, there isn't enough time to take out a new toy or build something new;

• waiting until everyone is dressed before going out on the playground;

• putting away the puzzle before starting another activity, or shutting off the tape player before leaving the listening center.

First Grade

1 Follows classroom rules and routines.

Six year olds follow rules and routines best when they have helped shape them and when rules are simple and consistent. Like five year olds, they can be quite dogmatic with their peers, insisting on adherence to rules that even they may sometimes forget. Although they are likely to need adult encouragement and reminders, some ways that six year olds demonstrate the ability to follow rules and routines are:

• locating and replacing personal belongings and classroom supplies;

• taking turns in group discussions;

• arriving in the morning and knowing what to do to begin the day's activities;

• knowing the daily schedule without continually asking "What's happening next?"

Second Grade

1 Follows classroom rules and routines.

Seven year olds follow rules and routines best when they have helped to shape them and when the rules remain consistent. Through classroom meetings and cooperative group work, second graders develop an understanding of respect and responsibility for the community. They demonstrate the ability to follow rules and routines by:

• locating and replacing personal belongings and classroom supplies independently;

• taking turns and listening respectfully to others in group discussions;

• getting a book and reading quietly during independent reading;

• knowing the daily and weekly classroom schedule and routine (times for music, physical education, or writing workshop).

Third Grade

1 Follows classroom rules and routines.

Third graders are more inclined to follow rules that they have helped to establish than those that are imposed on them. Through classroom meetings and cooperative group work, third graders develop an understanding of respect and responsibility for the community. Some ways they demonstrate the ability to follow rules and routines are:

• locating necessary materials and quickly starting work during work periods;

• reminding others of classroom rules and routines in supportive ways;

• knowing the daily and weekly schedule and routine (times for music, physical education, or writing workshop);

• following the rules for group discussions (taking turns, listening to the ideas of others, sticking to a topic).

Fourth Grade

1 Acts with responsibility and independence.

By nine years of age, children can be expected to be more self-reliant, having internalized school behaviors such as following rules and routines, managing transitions, and using materials carefully. They like predictable daily routines, but they can also be flexible about unexpected changes. Their emerging awareness of their physical self allows them to take greater responsibility for self-care and personal hygiene. Examples include:

• respecting and following classroom and school rules, and reminding others in respectful ways to do so;

• organizing information, time, work area, and materials (for example, being able to work on long-term projects with the appropriate materials, information, resources, and collaborators);

• assuming responsibility for personal work (completing homework and returning it to school, keeping track of assignments and projects);

• providing an accurate accounting of their participation and responsibility in events (problems occurring on the playground, small group discussions, science investigations).

Fifth Grade

1 Acts with responsibility and independence.

Ten year olds are becoming independent, dependable, and trustworthy. They should be able to negotiate the responsibilities of school work with only a few reminders. Most fifth graders can handle expected and unexpected transitions smoothly. They are more inclined to follow rules they have helped to establish rather than those imposed upon them, and it is important to them that everyone is held equally accountable for classroom rules. They can be expected to accept responsibility for personal hygiene. Examples include:

• adjusting with ease to a substitute teacher;

• following the rules for group discussions (listening to others, talking one at a time, being respectful when differences of opinion are aired);

• asking permission to use someone else's belongings and returning them when finished;

• being prepared for and anticipating activities in the daily schedule (having sneakers for gym, putting things away, and getting what is needed without reminders);

• accepting responsibility for their contribution to problems.

I Personal and Social Development

B Self control continued

Kindergarten

2 Uses classroom materials purposefully and respectfully.

One of the major challenges of school for five year olds is learning how to care for classroom materials. In school, a child learns how to use materials thoughtfully so that they continue to be available for others, and how to put things away so that others can easily find them. Examples include:

• using materials and equipment without breaking or destroying them;

• using materials with intention, such as playing the piano with a song in mind, not just pounding;

• hanging dress-up clothes on their proper hooks;

• using scissors appropriately for cutting, and then putting them back in their assigned place;

• keeping the sand inside the sand table;

• taking out the building blocks to create a structure rather than just emptying the shelves.

First Grade

2 Uses materials purposefully and respectfully.

Six year olds are learning to care for the property of others. After they have received direction on how to use materials appropriately, it is reasonable to expect they can do so with few reminders. Examples include:

• using markers, crayons, and scissors, and returning them to supply shelves or baskets when finished;

• finding and using the appropriate materials with intention (locating a magnifier to look more closely at butterfly wings or getting a bucket of unifix cubes to solve a math problem);

• assisting others with cleanup after finishing one's own.

Second Grade

2 Uses materials purposefully and respectfully.

Most second graders still need clear directions about how to use materials, but are growing in their ability to do so with independence and intention. Examples include:

• finding software for the computer and returning it to the proper storage place when finished;

• setting up paints and then cleaning up;

• storing adaptive equipment in places where it will not disrupt the flow of traffic (for example, placing crutches next to a chair when they are not in use);

• locating and using appropriate materials with intention (getting a ruler to draw a straight line or using Cuisenaire rods to solve a math problem involving multiplication);

• assisting others with cleanup after finishing one's own.

I   Personal and Social Development

Third Grade

2 Uses materials purposefully and respectfully.

Third graders need only minimal guidance to use materials with independence and intention. Learning responsible care and use of materials is an important aspect of participating in a positive learning climate. Examples of how third graders use materials with respect and purpose include:

• finding software for the computer and returning it to the proper storage place when finished;

• locating scissors, tape, and markers for a project and returning them when finished;

• asking permission to use someone else's belongings and then returning them;

• taking the classroom's soccer ball outside for recess and then returning it.

Fourth Grade

No equivalent performance indicator at this level.

Fifth Grade

No equivalent performance indicator at this level.

Kindergarten

3 Manages transitions and adapts to changes in routine.

Adapting to or accepting changes in routine is often difficult to learn. However, change is very much a part of growth. Five year olds are beginning to adjust to changes and learn that different situations call for different behaviors. Children show this flexibility by:

• moving smoothly from one routine to another (for example, from activity period to clean-up, or from story time to getting ready to go home);

• moving from home to school without extensive or long-lasting anxiety;

• greeting visitors who come into the classroom and then continuing with work;

• remembering to whisper when visiting the library.

First Grade

3 Manages transitions and adapts to changes in routine.

First graders rely on the predictability of routines. Adapting to or accepting change is often difficult for them. With adult support they can begin to handle change and recognize that different situations call for different behaviors. Some ways children demonstrate the ability to manage transitions and be flexible in behavior include:

• moving from one activity to another with minimal teacher guidance (for example, putting away journals and coming to a class meeting);

• leaving an unfinished task to complete at another time, for example, setting their journals aside and returning to them after lunch;

• hearing that gym time has been canceled and accepting that classroom game time will replace it.

Second Grade

3 Manages transitions and adjusts behavior to new places and unexpected events.

Second graders rely on the predictability of routines, and often show uncertainty when faced with changes and transitions (for example, shifts in schedule, taking trips, or special events). Ways that seven year olds show the ability to manage transitions and be flexible are:

• moving from one activity to another with minimal teacher guidance (such as coming in from outdoor recess and settling down for quiet reading);

• having to stop a woodworking project because choice time is over but accepting that it can be completed the next day;

• adjusting to changes in the classroom schedule and moving into new or unplanned activities with relative ease (accepting that because the graphing project is taking more time than expected, there will be no journal writing today).

Third Grade

3 Manages transitions and adjusts behavior to new places and unexpected events.

Although third graders rely on the predictability of routines, they are increasingly able to adjust to change with only minimal frustration. Some ways children demonstrate the ability to manage transitions and be flexible include:

• responding quickly to the teacher's request to put things away and get ready to work on math;

• adjusting to changes in the classroom schedule by moving into new or unplanned activities with ease (finding out a specialist is sick and that instead of art, the class will continue work on science activities);

• entering or exiting the building, gym, or cafeteria quietly, whether alone or in a group.

Fourth Grade

No equivalent performance indicator at this level.

Fifth Grade

No equivalent performance indicator at this level.

I Personal and Social Development

B Self control continued

Kindergarten

No equivalent performance indicator at this level.

First Grade

No equivalent performance indicator at this level.

Second Grade

No equivalent performance indicator at this level.

Third Grade

No equivalent performance indicator at this level.

Fourth Grade

2 **Uses coping strategies to manage a range of feelings and situations.**

By age nine, children are beginning to learn how to handle complex emotions such as frustration, praise, excitement, failure, and disappointment. With adult support they can begin to use coping strategies, which might include talking over a problem with a peer or adult, taking time out from frustrating activities, tackling alternative approaches, or trying something a second time. Examples include:

• being left out of a game and finding other people with whom to play;

• finding something really funny, laughing for awhile, and then knowing how to pull back and settle down;

• accepting compliments graciously from peers after sharing a project and then being able to move on to respond to the work of others.

Fifth Grade

2 **Uses coping strategies to manage a range of feelings and situations.**

Ten year olds are learning how to handle complex emotions such as frustration, praise, anger, excitement, failure, and disappointment. They continue to need supportive adults to listen to them and help them consider strategies, such as taking time out, tackling alternative approaches, or talking things over with adults or friends. Examples include:

• playing in a game despite not being selected by the better team;

• taking time out before trying to talk over disputes with peers;

• recognizing that the topic selected for a project is not working out, talking it over with the teacher, and moving on to a new plan;

• accepting praise from peers after sharing some work and then moving on to respond to the work of others.

I Personal and Social Development

C Approach to learning

Kindergarten

1 Shows eagerness and curiosity as a learner.

Five year olds are active learners and are curious and excited about their environment. They demonstrate curiosity in their play and can become very insistent when they have strong ideas. Examples include:

• being excited and curious about new things in the classroom, such as a collection of fall leaves or shells from the sea shore;

• asking meaningful and appropriate questions;

• showing interest in stories and events related by other children;

• looking at a picture of a castle and trying to build it with blocks.

First Grade

1 Shows eagerness and curiosity as a learner.

Because six year olds learn from direct experience, they are most likely to show interest and curiosity as learners in the context of active tasks. They demonstrate interest and curiosity in different ways, depending on their individual learning styles. Some children express themselves through art, construction, music, or dramatics, while others use words. Ways that six year olds show eagerness to learn include:

• seeking more specific information about a subject (looking in the class library for books about insects after going on a science walk to collect small creatures);

• making puppets based on a story read by the teacher and carefully working to capture the details of each character;

• contributing an anecdote to a class discussion based on something learned earlier;

• replicating at home an activity experienced in the classroom (for example, repeating a science experiment).

Second Grade

1 Shows eagerness and curiosity as a learner.

Seven year olds continue to learn primarily through direct experience, and are beginning to understand and express abstract ideas through pictures, words and symbolic forms. They demonstrate interest and curiosity as learners in different ways, depending on their own learning styles. Some children express themselves through art, construction, music, or dramatics, while others use verbal and written language. Ways that seven year olds show eagerness and curiosity about learning include:

• seeking additional information about objects and events in the classroom (looking for a book in the class library to answer a question about the class's hermit crab);

• pursuing an independent project with intensity, such as building a model of a suspension bridge after hearing about one in a story;

• returning daily to the science table to weigh classroom objects and keeping track of their weights.

Third Grade

1 Shows eagerness and curiosity as a learner.

Eight year olds are developing the ability to express and understand abstract ideas through pictures, words, and symbolic forms. Because children demonstrate interest and curiosity as learners in different ways, it is important to provide many means of expression. Some children express themselves through art, construction, music, or dramatics, while others use verbal and written language. Some ways that eight year olds show a positive attitude about learning include:

• exploring a special interest in some depth (a research project about the planets, reading a series of biographies about famous basketball players, or building an elaborate project);

• bringing in an article about a local environmental issue and wanting to follow up on it in some way (suggesting a class project, writing letters to local officials);

• recalling information from a family experience and applying it to a classroom activity.

Fourth Grade

1 Shows initiative and personal investment as a learner.

Children at this age express their interest in learning by actively engaging in work that they find important and meaningful. Nine year olds take initiative in areas of personal interest. Their interest in accomplishing tasks is accompanied by a beginning recognition of the processes involved, including organization, attention to detail, and, when necessary, revision. Their emerging study skills allow them to pursue more complex projects. Examples include:

• pursuing a special area of interest in some depth (for example, continuing to work on a math problem even though others have started recess);

• sharing ideas, opinions, talents, and skills with others (playing a musical instrument, bringing in a newspaper article about a current event to share with the class);

• using personal time to complete unfinished work (reading a book or working on a project);

• extending a teacher-initiated activity into a self-directed activity (following up a science lesson with an independent investigation of the same topic).

Fifth Grade

1 Shows initiative and personal investment as a learner.

Fifth graders easily immerse themselves in work that is personally meaningful. As they become more skilled in using reference materials and peer resources, they rely less on teachers and become more independent in their learning. Examples of students' personal investment and initiative include:

• willingness to use a variety of resources independently (teachers, librarians, experts in the field, organizations that relate to interest areas);

• researching and presenting a personal interest area in depth (through writing, creating models, oral presentations);

• sharing ideas, talents, and skills with others (playing a musical instrument, bringing in newspaper articles about current events to share with the class);

• presenting work that demonstrates prior planning;

• using leisure time to complete work (reading a books, completing projects, working on math problems).

I Personal and Social Development

C Approach to learning continued

Kindergarten	First Grade	Second Grade
2 Chooses new as well as a variety of familiar classroom activities.	**2 Begins to make independent choices of materials, activities, and work/play partners.**	**2 Makes independent choices of materials, activities, and work/play partners.**

Kindergarten

2 Chooses new as well as a variety of familiar classroom activities.

Although some children this age repeatedly choose familiar activities and are hesitant to venture into new areas, others are very willing to try new experiences or to take risks. Examples of making independent choices include:

• selecting new activities during choice time, such as trying the carpentry table or the computer for the first time;

• showing excitement about new opportunities and experiences presented in the classroom (such as a new floor puzzle the teacher introduced during group discussion);

• choosing to play or work on a project because the activity interests them, rather than because friends are doing it.

First Grade

2 Begins to make independent choices of materials, activities, and work/play partners.

First graders may have preferences about what they like to do, and how and with whom they want to do it. When given the opportunity to make choices in the classroom, six year olds can make some independent choices of familiar as well as unfamiliar activities and experiences. Examples of how first graders demonstrate their ability to make choices include:

• deciding what to write about during writing workshop;

• making an independent choice of material from the math shelf to help solve a problem;

• participating in a newly introduced classroom or recess activity;

• deciding to work on a second choice of activity during choice time because others have already selected their first choice.

Second Grade

2 Makes independent choices of materials, activities, and work/play partners.

For second graders, making independent choices includes the willingness to try new experiences as well as making choices independent of adults. Some ways they demonstrate their ability to make independent choices include:

• selecting a second choice of activity when the first choice is unavailable;

• trying to write poetry for the first time instead of again doing a narrative during writing workshop;

• working with blocks or Legos during a free-choice time, even if there are no other girls doing so;

• participating in a newly introduced classroom or recess activity;

• feeling comfortable when choosing a new chapter book from the class library;

• making a work plan and getting started on it (deciding what to paint or which software to use).

Third Grade

2 Makes independent choices of materials, activities, and work/play partners.

For third graders, this skill includes knowing how to generate options, weighing pros and cons, and recognizing that attempting something new tends to cause initial discomfort. Some ways third graders demonstrate their ability to make independent choices include:

• evaluating the benefits and drawbacks prior to deciding on a project;

• trying something for the first time (for example, using the word-processing program on the computer);

• making a work plan and getting started on it (choosing the role to play in a skit, or a topic for a story);

• finding three library books and then deciding which one to take out;

• reviewing activity options during indoor recess or free-choice time and then deciding to continue writing a story begun during writer's workshop.

Fourth Grade

2 Sets personal goals and is self-reflective.

When given the opportunity to reflect upon themselves and their work, fourth graders can begin to set personal goals and evaluate their efforts. They are learning to articulate why a piece of work is successful or where it needs further attention. They can also think about how their attitudes and social and personal choices affect their learning. Some examples of this include:

• writing in a journal about school life (participation in group projects, interactions with peers, things they would like to research);

• deciding to sit next to someone with whom they will not fool around;

• discussing a piece of writing with a peer, parent, or teacher in terms of its organization, clarity of expression, or amount of effort expended;

• setting goals for the week, quarter, or year (to make a friend, follow directions better, complete work, participate more in class, improve writing).

Fifth Grade

2 Sets personal goals and is self-reflective.

Through teacher modeling and regular opportunities to reflect upon their attitudes, work habits, and products, fifth graders learn to assess their own progress and goals. They can articulate why a piece of work was successful or where it needs more clarity, detail, and depth. They can set goals related to personal and social choices that they make during the school day. Some examples of this kind of self-reflection include:

• writing and reflecting in a journal about school or home life (participation in group projects, peer interactions, family changes);

• personally evaluating work (in terms of organization, clarity, appearance, accuracy, personal investment);

• setting goals for the week, quarter, year (to make a friend, follow directions better, complete work, participate more in class, improve writing).

■ Personal and Social Development

C Approach to learning continued

Kindergarten	First Grade	Second Grade
3 Approaches tasks with flexibility and inventiveness.	**3 Approaches tasks with flexibility and inventiveness.**	**3 Approaches tasks with flexibility and inventiveness.**

Kindergarten

3 Approaches tasks with flexibility and inventiveness.

Five year olds often need help and encouragement when trying different ways of accomplishing a task. Many children are reluctant to try new ideas because if they do not succeed the result is often interpreted negatively by themselves or adults. Trial and error nurtures and encourages creativity. After children have tried unsuccessfully to solve problems it is important for them to know when and where to get help. Some examples of flexibility and risk taking include:

• attempting several different ways to solve a problem (for example, trying to build a roof over a structure with different types of blocks);

• attempting several ways of folding or cutting paper to make a kite or airplane;

• communicating frustration in an acceptable way after failing to accomplish a task;

• creating something new (for example, a pretend camera) by combining several familiar materials (for example, a milk carton and tape).

First Grade

3 Approaches tasks with flexibility and inventiveness.

First graders who are flexible and inventive can tackle problems with an open mind, try several different approaches, and seek help when they are stuck. Sometimes, inventiveness is expressed through imaginative play. Examples of how first graders demonstrate their flexibility and inventiveness include:

• using materials in new ways (using unifix cubes as weight units on a balance scale);

• building a structure with blocks or Legos and then using it for dramatic play;

• mixing paint to come up with greater color variety;

• bringing color cubes from the math shelves into the block area to use as floor tiles in a building.

Second Grade

3 Approaches tasks with flexibility and inventiveness.

Flexible thinkers in a second grade classroom tackle problems with an open mind, try different approaches, consider alternative ideas, and know when to seek help. Examples of how second graders demonstrate flexibility and inventiveness include:

• finding a way to pursue a personal interest (for example, animals) within the parameters of whatever activity they might choose (selecting books about animals, or writing a story and drawing pictures of animals);

• considering different ways to measure classroom dimensions (using lengths of string, a trundle wheel, or Cuisenaire rods);

• inventing new ways to play familiar games.

I Personal and Social Development

Third Grade

3 Approaches tasks with flexibility and inventiveness.

Flexible and inventive third graders are likely to tackle problems with an open mind, try different approaches, consider alternative ideas, and know when to seek help. Examples of how third graders demonstrate flexibility and inventiveness include:

• reflecting on a task to consider alternatives before getting started (pondering a few choices for a story before beginning to write);

• letting go of reliable estimating and counting methods and experimenting with new ones (instead of counting by twos, deciding to count by tens);

• bringing a problem to the class to hear many ideas and then selecting one to try (finding an ending to a story).

Fourth Grade

3 Approaches tasks with flexibility and inventiveness.

Although willing to tackle new experiences, many fourth graders are likely to think that there is only one way to solve a problem and that each problem has only one right answer. Through class discussions and demonstrations, nine year olds can explore and experience various ways of approaching academic, personal and social problems. Examples include:

• attempting to solve a math problem, then remembering a similar problem and applying a similar strategy;

• considering the alternatives before getting started on a task;

• listening to and critically evaluating other people's ideas;

• considering more than one idea as a possible solution to a problem;

• discussing different ways to find information (going to the library, talking to experts, asking friends).

Fifth Grade

3 Approaches tasks with flexibility and inventiveness.

When ten year olds feel a sense of ownership about problems or projects, they think and solve problems with flexibility and inventiveness. They can seek ideas from many sources, including books, peers, and adults. Examples include:

• letting go of a reliable method and experimenting with a new one;

• being excited by a building project and drawing a variety of plans to test out ideas;

• examining situations from several points of view;

• seeing that something does not work, posing questions, and then extending or redirecting thinking.

▌Personal and Social Development
C Approach to learning continued

Kindergarten	First Grade	Second Grade
4 Sustains attention to a task over a period of time, even after encountering problems.	**4 Sustains attention to work over a period of time.**	**4 Sustains attention to work over a period of time.**

Kindergarten

Five year olds often become frustrated when tasks require skills that are beyond their abilities. They may need encouragement to keep trying and to develop persistence. They may also need support to understand that making mistakes or failing the first few times are important parts of learning and gaining skills. Some examples include:

• making several attempts at solving a problem (for example, assembling a new puzzle, or gluing together a three-dimensional collage);

• remembering on a day-to-day basis to maintain long-term projects (such as watering seeds regularly, recording corn plant growth on a chart daily, reading the thermometer and recording temperatures regularly);

• continuing projects from one day to the next, such as working on a clay sculpture for several days.

First Grade

Six year olds tend to begin more projects and activities than they complete. They will more readily persist with projects that especially interest them. Examples of how six year olds demonstrate their ability to sustain interest over time include:

• returning repeatedly to the math center to work with tangrams in an effort to create a square;

• choosing to work on a jigsaw puzzle for several consecutive days;

• putting away a story and returning to work on it the next day;

• going to the library repeatedly to get books related to the class's study of animals.

Second Grade

Seven year olds are increasingly able to concentrate for longer periods of time and often want to complete the projects they begin. They can be impatient with themselves as they strive for perfection, and sometimes have difficulty understanding that accomplishment often comes with practice and a number of failures. Some ways that seven year olds show their ability to sustain interest in work include:

• running out of time when constructing an intricately complex pattern block design, and returning the next day to recreate the design and add to it;

• staying with a chapter book until it is completed;

• working on one story in a journal or a writing folder for several days;

• finding materials related to the topic the class is studying (bringing in books on the subject from home or the library).

Third Grade

4 Sustains attention to work over a period of time.

By the time children are eight, their capacity to be self-motivated is emerging and they can sustain work for extended periods of time. They often want to complete tasks and tend to do so in a rush, unless they feel personally invested in something. Examples of how third graders show their ability to sustain interest include:

• working on a challenging math problem for several days in a row;

• making a diorama for a book report that requires work outside of school;

• taking on and completing a multi-step computer project over the course of several work periods;

• reading several books by the same author;

• spending several days working on an art project.

Fourth Grade

4 Sustains attention to work for a period of time.

Nine year olds gradually immerse themselves in individual tasks for longer periods of time. As they develop personal standards for their work, their attention to the task and its detail is extended. Examples include:

• revising a piece of work instead of giving up on it or throwing it away;

• persisting in tasks that are self-directed as well as those initiated by others;

• completing work that require time outside of school.

Fifth Grade

4 Chooses to use time constructively and works in a focused manner.

Ten year olds continue to develop the capacity to immerse themselves in a piece of work for increasingly longer periods of time. They can look at their work objectively, determine the quality they would like to aspire to, and then work toward it. Examples include:

• revising work instead of giving up or discarding it;

• persisting in tasks that are self-directed as well as those initiated by others;

• working in a group or with a partner in a focused manner;

• using resources outside of school to enrich school projects.

I Personal and Social Development

D Interaction with others

Kindergarten

1 Interacts easily with one or more children when playing or working cooperatively.

Five year old children are beginning to learn how to play cooperatively with one or more children, listen to peers, and arrive at solutions in a cooperative manner. Some five year olds still find it difficult to interact with peers they do not know very well. These children often need teacher encouragement to try activities with a new group of children. Evidence that children are developing these skills includes:

• following suggestions given by a friend about how to proceed in their play (for example, deciding to build a fire station with the large hollow blocks, in response to a friend's suggestion);

• giving assistance to peers who are trying to solve a problem (helping to zip coats or tie shoes, or figuring out how to divide the Legos among three children);

• choosing to work with new children;

• helping a friend set the snack table with napkins and cups.

First Grade

1 Interacts easily with peers when playing or working cooperatively.

Six year olds want to socialize with peers but often lack the skills to do so effectively. They often need adult guidance and support. Examples of a six year old child's ease with interactions include:

• readily sitting with a group of children at the lunch or snack table;

• giving and receiving peer assistance during work times (for example, helping someone figure out the spelling of a word);

• suggesting that someone join a group in order to share the markers;

• working cooperatively with several children on a math task structured by the teacher.

Second Grade

1 Interacts easily with peers when playing or working cooperatively.

Seven year olds tend to work, play, and interact more cooperatively and successfully when they have initiated the activity or selected their partners. They also often want time to work alone. Examples of how seven year olds demonstrate their ability to interact cooperatively include:

• giving and receiving assistance on a group project (building a model, playing a computer game, recording science observations);

• letting others join games that are already underway;

• working cooperatively on a group project initiated by a teacher (a book group, research task, or making graphs);

• initiating conversation with a new student and showing her/him around the school.

Third Grade

1 Interacts easily with peers when playing or working cooperatively.

Third graders are actively learning about themselves in relation to their peers. Developing close friendships is often very important at this age. Some ways that third graders show they can interact easily and cooperatively include:

• playing with a best friend at choice time or recess and letting a third person join in;

• considering how to change an activity so a physically challenged classmate can participate;

• cooperating in groups or pairs on teacher-initiated tasks (working on math problems, creating skits and puppet shows, or completing a social studies research report);

• welcoming a new player into a game that has already begun;

• assuming both leader and follower roles in group activities.

Fourth Grade

1 Begins to maintain close friendships without excluding others.

Fourth graders maintain long-lasting friendships and tend to select same-sex friends. At times they may find themselves in situations that exclude others. Their own need to feel as if they belong can leave others feeling left out. The nine year old's sense of fairness and concern for others helps balance their personal needs with group needs. Examples include:

• feeling secure enough in a friendship to invite a third person to join an activity;

• initiating or sustaining a conversation with a "new" person;

• choosing someone other than a best friend to work with.

Fifth Grade

1 Maintains close friendships without excluding others.

By the time students are in fifth grade, friendships are of primary importance. Many tend to stay with the same friends, leave others out, and neglect the feelings of the excluded. Examples of their ability to manage social relationships include:

• welcoming new players to games or group activities already underway;

• choosing to work with different people during the day;

• having a best friend in the class and being open to other students.

I Personal and Social Development

D Interaction with others continued

Kindergarten	First Grade	Second Grade

2 Interacts easily with familiar adults.

Many five year old children are more comfortable talking and interacting with adults than with their peers. Feeling at ease with adults includes:

• greeting the teacher or other adults when arriving in the morning;

• relating events and anecdotes to the teacher with ease and comfort;

• interacting easily with other adults in the school, such as the custodian, the lunch room monitor, or the crossing guard.

2 Interacts easily with adults.

At six, children are beginning to change their relationships with adults. They are working toward greater independence, but they want adults close by for approval and support. They demonstrate skills in this area by:

• bringing their homework to the teacher and soliciting an opinion;

• telling the teacher about yesterday's family expedition;

• responding appropriately to greetings from teachers or other adults when arriving in the morning;

• participating in informal conversations with adults during snack time or lunch.

2 Interacts easily with adults.

By seven, relationships with adults are becoming more independent, although they still want adults close by for approval and support. Examples of how seven year olds show their comfort with adults are:

• communicating about problems with teachers, assistants, resource teachers, or volunteers;

• responding appropriately to greetings from teachers or other adults when arriving in the morning;

• communicating with a teacher about a story and getting some ideas about possible endings;

• bringing a teacher's note to the office and being able to talk briefly with the school secretary;

• talking with a museum guide about an exhibit on a class trip.

Third Grade

2 Interacts easily with adults.

Eight year olds are becoming increasingly independent; they enjoy interactions with adults if they do not feel they are being too controlled by them. Examples of ways eight year olds demonstrate comfortable interactions with adults are:

• inviting the teacher to be the fourth player in a board game;

• solving problems with the help of the teacher, an assistant, or the physical education teacher;

• asking the teacher to make a book recommendation;

• volunteering to help the teacher with organizational tasks (stapling, collating, or preparing materials for a project);

• responding appropriately to greetings from teachers or other adults when arriving in the morning.

Fourth Grade

2 Interacts easily with adults.

Fourth graders are becoming increasingly independent of adults and require less direct supervision than younger students. They will often look to adults for support and guidance, to assist them in a task, or to share some of their work. Ways that a student demonstrates comfortable interactions with adults include:

• using a journal to ask a teacher for personal advice;

• using adults as resources (for example, to help with work, recommend books, discuss problems);

• volunteering to help adults with classroom organization (collating, stapling, preparing materials for projects);

• sharing work done outside the classroom with another teacher (an art project, a math problem done with another class, a peer-tutoring activity);

• agreeing to and abiding by consequences set by the adult;

• inviting the teacher to join in a game.

Fifth Grade

2 Interacts easily with adults.

Ten year olds are more involved with their peers than with adults. While attempting to separate themselves from adults, they also look to them for support and encouragement. When advice or comfort is needed, they still seek trustworthy adults. Some ways that ten year olds demonstrate comfortable interactions with adults include:

• engaging in conversations about problems;

• asking for confidential advice from a teacher (in a journal, after school, during a conference);

• using adults as resources (for example, to help with some work, recommend books, discuss problems);

• volunteering to help adults with classroom tasks (collating, stapling, preparing materials for a project);

• agreeing to and abiding by consequences set by adults.

I Personal and Social Development

D Interaction with others continued

Kindergarten

3 Participates in the group life of the class.

Five year olds are fairly adept at following group expectations if they have had previous school experience. They are very interested in the meaning of friendship: "What does having a friend mean?", "how does friendship work?" This interest helps them become involved in the group because they want to be with their friends. Five year olds are also anxious to establish order in their lives and prefer consistent routines. This "order" gives them a sense of control. Five year olds show their understanding of group life by:

• taking part in group activities, such as circle, music, or story time;

• showing knowledge of class routines (for example, that snack comes after cleanup, and quiet reading time after snack);

• remembering to wash hands before a cooking project;

• putting toys and manipulatives away in their proper places when finished, before going on to a new activity;

• helping a friend find a lost toy;

• listening to a discussion and participating in developing an idea or plan.

First Grade

3 Participates in the group life of the class.

Six year olds are beginning to identify with groups as well as understanding how groups function. They are gradually learning to take turns, share, and listen to others. At this age children begin to understand why groups need rules. Examples of how six year olds demonstrate the ability to participate in groups are:

• listening and participating at a school assembly;

• listening to classmates' ideas during group discussions;

• making contributions to group efforts, such as making props for a class play;

• completing classroom jobs without being reminded.

Second Grade

3 Participates in the group life of the class.

Seven year olds are learning how to work in groups and how groups function. Group life is becoming increasingly important to them as they identify more with peers. Ways they demonstrate skills in this area are:

• participating willingly as an active player or audience member in group events (in class games, at assemblies);

• considering the ideas of others when making group plans (how to construct pulleys during science activity, or making a class newspaper);

• helping others complete classroom jobs after their own are done, so that everything is ready by day's end;

• helping to plan a special event.

Third Grade

3 **Participates in the group life of the class and school.**

Third graders have a growing sense of community, which is beginning to extend beyond their classroom. Wanting very much to feel included, they focus on learning how to work in groups and how groups function. Some examples of how they participate in the group life of the class and school are:

• making contributions to group efforts (a class bake sale, a recycling project);

• considering the ideas of others when making group plans;

• representing the class on an all-school committee;

• assuming a leadership role in class activities when necessary.

Fourth Grade

3 **Works cooperatively and collaboratively in classroom and school activities.**

Fourth graders' growing sense of community includes knowing how to assume the roles of leader and follower. They are beginning to understand why groups need structure and rules to function effectively. At this age they can communicate, share resources, and influence one another in a positive manner when working in groups. Examples include:

• representing the class on an all-school council;

• making meaningful contributions to group projects;

• fulfilling roles in cooperative learning groups (being the group facilitator, note taker, presenter);

• playing fairly in outdoor games and knowing when to take a leadership or follower role.

Fifth Grade

3 **Works cooperatively and collaboratively in group activities.**

When ten year olds are provided with opportunities to work cooperatively in the classroom and school, they can effectively communicate, sharing ideas and resources. They can be expected to show some flexibility in assuming the roles of leader or participant. Examples of students working cooperatively and collaboratively include:

• going along with group ideas, even when they differ from their own;

• participating in class projects or performances;

• sharing ideas and taking an active role in cooperative learning groups (being the group facilitator, note taker, or presenter when brainstorming ideas for a specific project);

• contributing to a group effort (fundraising and recycling projects, schoolyard cleanup);

• participating in some form of school service (peer tutoring, student council, school mediator, cafeteria helper, recycling team member).

I Personal and Social Development

D Interaction with others continued

Kindergarten	First Grade	Second Grade
4 Participates and follows rules in group activities.	**4 Plays cooperatively in group games.**	**4 Plays cooperatively and fairly in group games.**

Kindergarten

Winning is not usually as important to five year olds as using and learning the skills involved in playing a game. Five year olds are more concerned with how well they can play rather than being the best. Five year olds show the ability to play cooperatively by:

• participating in simple, noncompetitive games, like The Hokey Pokey;

• waiting for turns;

• adapting to and playing cooperatively in situations where the rules are established at the beginning of play;

• playing simple card games like Go Fish or Concentration;

• playing listening and guessing games like I Spy;

• joining a small group going to the library;

• being a part of the audience as well as an active participant in group events.

First Grade

Six year olds tend to be competitive. However, while they may invent their own rules for games, want to be first, and even expect to win, they are often very concerned about fairness. Six year olds learn the skills of cooperative game playing best with games that do not involve winning and losing. Examples of how six year olds demonstrate skills in this area include:

• tolerating that they will have to wait for a turn in guessing games that involve the whole class (for example, "I am thinking of a number");

• while playing a board game, watching other players take their turns instead of roaming around the classroom;

• taking turns fairly in games with two or three players;

• participating in games with rules that involve winning and losing (bingo, Connect Four, checkers) with one or two other players.

Second Grade

Seven year olds are developing the ability to play cooperatively and fairly in games with rules although they tend to need opportunities to discuss and debate the rules. It is often easier for them to manage competition and fairness issues when groups are small. Examples of how seven year olds demonstrate the ability to play cooperatively and fairly include:

• participating in board games and card games without becoming angry or discouraged;

• going along with the rest of the group when playing a game, even when the group's ideas differ from their own;

• working with one or two others to invent a new game or create a variation on an existing game;

• helping a group get organized for a playground game (soccer, kickball, jump rope) and then participating in it.

Third Grade

4 Plays cooperatively and fairly in group games.

Playing fairly and cooperatively for third graders includes taking turns, watching the actions of others even when it isn't one's turn, negotiating rules, and beginning to handle losing without anger. Eight year olds often need to discuss and debate the outcomes of competitive games. Some ways they demonstrate cooperative and fair play are:

• participating competently in games with rules (board games, card games, kickball), and managing feelings of frustration reasonably well;

• going along with the rest of the group when playing, even when the ideas differ from their own (about rule interpretations, about whether a ball was actually out);

• participating in outdoor games (soccer, softball, tag) and knowing when to be a leader or follower.

Fourth Grade

No equivalent performance indicator at this level.

Fifth Grade

No equivalent performance indicator at this level.

I Personal and Social Development

I Personal and Social Development

D Interaction with others continued

Kindergarten	First Grade	Second Grade
5 Shows empathy and caring for others.	**5 Shows empathy and caring for others.**	**5 Shows empathy and caring for others.**

Kindergarten

Some children naturally express care and understanding for others' feelings. Other children need guidance and support from teachers to acquire these qualities. Children show empathy and understanding by:

• displaying sadness along with a friend whose pet has died;

• being concerned and wanting to help when a classmate falls and hurts her/himself;

• showing concern for a friend who has been excluded from a game or dramatic play;

• trying to help when a classmate's block structure has fallen;

• helping a classmate pick up spilled crayons;

• carrying something for a child who is unable to do so.

First Grade

Some children naturally show caring and empathy for others while others need adult and peer guidance to acquire these qualities. Many six year olds are quite egocentric and, therefore, it is difficult for them to consider other viewpoints. Examples of how six year olds show empathy and caring include:

• staying inside at recess to keep an injured friend company;

• helping a peer rebuild a block structure that was knocked down;

• expressing concern for someone experiencing a problem (the death of a pet, a newcomer trying to adapt to the class).

Second Grade

Seven year olds are just beginning to consider others' viewpoints. Some children this age naturally show caring and empathy while others need guidance and support from adults and peers to acquire these qualities. Examples of how seven year olds show empathy and caring include:

• staying inside at recess to keep an injured friend company;

• helping a peer with a difficult assignment, even if it means missing the opportunity to do something new;

• expressing concern for someone experiencing a problem (an accident, a death in the family, a fire at home);

• finding ways to include less popular peers in group activities.

Third Grade

5 Shows empathy and caring for others.

As eight year olds become less egocentric, they can understand and empathize with others who seem at a disadvantage (such as peers with lower reading or athletic capabilities). By this age, children can be expected to consider other viewpoints. Examples of how eight year olds show empathy and caring include:

• expressing concern for peers experiencing problems (an accident, a death in the family, a fire at home);

• expressing concern and interest about a community problem (homelessness, pollution) through comments made during group discussions;

• considering the needs of a classmate with a disability (for example, holding a door open for a classmate in a wheelchair or remembering to face a hearing-impaired classmate when speaking);

• finding a way to include less popular peers in group activities.

Fourth Grade

4 Considers others' viewpoints and feelings.

As nine year olds become less egocentric they develop an appreciation for other people's worth and begin to understand and empathize with their concerns. Although they want to be heard and understood, they also can listen to others' thoughts and feelings. Examples include:

• discussing a current event and representing both sides;

• initiating positive comments to peers who generally have a difficult time fitting into the class;

• listening to peers during conflicts without interrupting;

• using body language that communicates respectful listening;

• participating in discussions that address social issues in the world (environmental problems, famines, homelessness);

• documenting their response to simulations that explore being different (being blindfolded while making a sandwich, playing a ball game while wearing a splint, learning a song or short story in sign language).

Fifth Grade

4 Considers others' viewpoints and feelings.

Intellectually, fifth graders are capable of reasoning and understanding multiple viewpoints. Socially, they often feel compelled to view issues as their friends do. When provided with a classroom atmosphere where mutual respect is modeled and feelings are discussed openly and safely, ten year olds can demonstrate tolerance and appreciation for different viewpoints and feelings. Some examples include:

• analyzing pieces of literature and defending the different viewpoints of particular characters;

• listening to peers without interrupting during a conflict;

• paraphrasing what another individual said during a discussion;

• participating in discussions that address social/political issues in the world (hunger, poverty, dictatorships).

I Personal and Social Development

E Conflict resolution

Kindergarten

1 **Seeks adult help when needed to resolve conflicts.**

Children this age still need instruction and guidance from adults about strategies for resolving conflict. Children show they are learning these skills by:

• asking for help when a second child wants to use the same blocks;

• using words suggested by an adult to settle conflicts;

• using compromise when intruded upon (for example, when a new child wants to enter a game already underway, making room for him or her during an appropriate break).

First Grade

No equivalent performance indicator at this level.

Second Grade

No equivalent performance indicator at this level.

Third Grade

No equivalent performance indicator at this level.

Fourth Grade

No equivalent performance indicator at this level.

Fifth Grade

No equivalent performance indicator at this level.

I Personal and Social Development

E Conflict resolution continued

Kindergarten	First Grade	Second Grade

Kindergarten

2 Uses words to resolve conflicts.

Using words and strategies to resolve conflicts — for example, "fair trades" or taking turns by mutual agreement — is an emerging skill for five year olds. They still need adult support and modeling to use words to solve problems, suggest possible solutions, and participate in compromise. They show that they are gaining these skills by:

• settling a dispute with another child through negotiation, addressing their own rights as well as accommodating the other child's needs (for example, "I'll use the paste for these two pieces of paper and then give it to you");

• taking turns without pushing or other conflict;

• sharing without grabbing;

• using words to express feelings, such as, "I don't like it when you push me."

First Grade

1 Begins to use discussion and compromise to resolve conflicts.

For six year olds, using words and strategies to resolve conflicts is an emerging skill. They tend to be upset easily when things do not go their way. Some examples of how they demonstrate their growing ability in this area include:

• negotiating with another child, using words that address one's own rights as well as the feelings of the other person;

• seeing other points of view or tolerating differences in viewpoints;

• discussing with two other children how to include a new member in their game;

• negotiating who will be first in line for the water fountain without being aggressive.

Second Grade

1 Uses discussion and compromise to resolve conflicts.

By seven, provided children have discussed conflict resolution, they can often resolve problems with words and strategies. Because fairness is so important to seven year olds, they often need a great deal of time to discuss and debate disagreements. Some examples of how they demonstrate the ability to use discussion and compromise include:

• negotiating with another child about how to use a computer program;

• discussing with a peer the pros and cons of using different methods to signify water in a river model, and then deciding on a method agreeable to both;

• communicating with two other players about how to include newcomers in their activities.

Third Grade

1 Uses discussion and compromise to resolve conflicts.

Eight year olds can use words and strategies to resolve conflicts, although the intensity of their emotions can sometimes interfere. Some examples of growth in this area are:

• negotiating with another child using words that defend one's personal rights and beliefs;

• seeing another's point of view or tolerating differences in viewpoint;

• bringing up a problem that occurs outside the classroom (in the gym or at recess) for class discussion.

Fourth Grade

1 Uses discussion and compromise to resolve conflicts.

Children of this age are exploring their ability to negotiate conflicts without relying on an adult. It is important to nine year olds that both sides of an issue be aired. When provided with opportunities that model appropriate interpersonal skills, students can discuss strategies and role play various problems that are relevant to them. Examples of growth include:

• attempting to implement a specific strategy for solving conflicts;

• negotiating with another student by using words to defend one's personal rights and beliefs and by considering the feelings of the other person;

• bringing a problem that occurs outside the classroom to a class meeting for discussion;

• stating one's own perspective and listening to others.

Fifth Grade

1 Uses discussion and compromise to resolve conflicts.

Ten year olds want to resolve their own conflicts, although the intensity of their emotions sometimes interferes with their ability to do this successfully. They are able to learn structured processes for resolving conflicts. When provided with opportunities that model appropriate interpersonal skills, students can discuss strategies and role play various problems that are relevant to them. Some examples of the ability to discuss and use compromise to resolve conflicts include:

• negotiating with another student by using words to defend one's personal rights and beliefs and by considering the feelings of the other person;

• stating one's own perspective and listening to others;

• bringing problems that occur outside the classroom to a class meeting and generating options for resolving them.

I Personal and Social Development

E Conflict resolution continued

Kindergarten	First Grade	Second Grade
No equivalent performance indicator at this level.	2 Seeks help when unable to resolve conflicts independently.	2 Seeks help and uses suggestions when unable to resolve conflicts independently.

Kindergarten

No equivalent performance indicator at this level.

First Grade

2 **Seeks help when unable to resolve conflicts independently.**

Six year olds are still in need of instruction and guidance from adults about strategies for resolving conflicts. Knowing when it is necessary to ask for help (rather than reacting impulsively) is an indication of a child's desire to have positive relationships. Examples of how children demonstrate their ability to get help include:

• seeking teacher assistance when game participants cannot agree on the rules;

• dealing with feelings of anger by using the words suggested by an adult;

• seeking teacher advice about a problem with a friend and then using the strategy discussed.

Second Grade

2 **Seeks help and uses suggestions when unable to resolve conflicts independently.**

Knowing when to ask for help and being able to use it is a sign of maturity in the seven year old. Examples of how they do this include:

• seeking teacher assistance when a project work group encounters seemingly irreconcilable differences;

• accepting help from an adult other than the teacher (paraprofessional, special subject teacher) when dealing with feelings of anger;

• using class meetings as a forum to help resolve interpersonal conflicts (turn-taking rules, problems at recess).

Third Grade

2 Seeks help and uses suggestions when unable to resolve conflicts independently.

By eight years of age, children can learn to rely on various strategies for conflict resolution, including getting help from an adult or peer, or using class meetings as a forum for problem solving. Examples of how they do this include:

• seeking and accepting help from an adult or a peer when dealing with feelings of anger;

• using class meetings as a forum to help resolve interpersonal conflicts (turn-taking rules, problems at recess);

• using previously suggested methods of conflict resolution during heated arguments.

Fourth Grade

2 Seeks help and uses suggestions when unable to resolve conflicts independently.

Even though nine year olds are learning how to resolve conflicts, they continue to need adult help when unsuccessful in resolving conflicts independently. It is important that children know how to request help from a variety of people (different adults, school counselor, peers, class meeting participants). Examples of a student's ability to seek help include:

• seeking the help of a teacher (or other mediator) when experiencing seemingly irreconcilable differences;

• accepting help from a peer or an adult when dealing with feelings of anger;

• using the help that is offered and calling upon previous suggestions to resolve conflicts.

Fifth Grade

2 Seeks help and uses suggestions when unable to resolve conflicts independently.

Even though ten year olds are learning various strategies to resolve conflicts independently, they sometimes need adult or peer assistance when unable to settle disputes. Examples include:

• seeking the help of teachers or other mediators when confronted with seemingly irreconcilable differences;

• accepting help from peers or adults when dealing with anger;

• using offered help and previous suggestions to resolve conflicts.

I Personal and Social Development

Language and Literacy

This domain emphasizes the acquisition of language skills to convey and interpret meaning. All of the components integrate multiple skills, rather than isolated abilities. The indicators in this domain reflect the belief that children learn to read and write the same way they learn to speak — naturally and slowly, using increasingly accurate approximations of adult norms.

II Language and Literacy
A Listening

Kindergarten	First Grade	Second Grade

Kindergarten

1 Listens for meaning in discussions and conversations.

At five years, children are beginning to pay increased attention to conversations and instructions that are not directed solely to them. Some children have a more difficult time listening to group instructions and discussions. Children who are hearing impaired may express understanding through body language, use of signs, head nodding, pointing, and other physical methods. Children demonstrate their developing skills in this area by:

• understanding teacher directions given to the class without needing immediately to ask the teacher what is to be done;

• recognizing the intent behind the words of peers, such as an apology given for causing an accident;

• showing understanding during a group discussion through body language (leaning forward) or facial expressions (a frown or a smile);

• understanding the message or story expressed in a video.

First Grade

1 Listens for meaning in discussions and conversations.

Six year olds are acquiring the ability to listen to the ideas of others and to listen as a way of gaining information. Because interest is a key factor in their listening ability, six year olds easily listen for pleasure and enjoyment. They can often sit for extended periods of time listening to a "good" story, but will squirm and fidget if asked to attend to something that does not immediately capture their interest. Examples of how they demonstrate listening skills include:

• responding appropriately to a presentation (for example, asking a relevant question after listening to a friend's story);

• demonstrating attentiveness as a listener through body language or facial expression;

• hearing a story about a family that moves to a different country and relating a personal anecdote;

• retelling what is heard after a story is read aloud or following another kind of presentation.

Second Grade

1 Listens for meaning in discussions and conversations.

For the seven year old, listening for meaning includes listening to ideas of others, listening as a way to gain information, and listening for pleasure and enjoyment. Seven year olds are beginning to ask specific questions to clarify or extend meaning. Examples of how they demonstrate their listening skills include:

• demonstrating attentiveness as a listener through body language or facial expressions;

• watching a video as part of a social studies lesson and then incorporating some of its details into stories they are writing;

• asking a question for clarification after listening to a classmate's story;

• reflecting on what is heard and relating personal experiences that are relevant to it.

Third Grade

1 Listens for meaning in discussions and conversations.

Eight year olds can listen attentively (for example, focus on the speaker and not interrupt) in a variety of situations, including listening to the ideas of others, as a way of gaining information, and for pleasure and enjoyment. Eight year olds can ask specific questions to clarify or extend meaning. Examples of how they demonstrate their listening skills include:

• asking for clarification of a classmate's idea, just shared during a group discussion;

• paraphrasing classmates' viewpoints expressed during a conflict;

• reflecting on what is heard and relating personal experiences that are relevant to it;

• listening to a visiting artist describe how a sculpture was made and then trying to incorporate those techniques into their own work.

Fourth Grade

1 Listens for meaning and to gain information in discussions and conversations.

Fourth graders can listen in a focused manner for extended periods of time. They can follow the plot when listening to stories or plays. They are gaining the skills needed to evaluate what is heard, connect it to prior knowledge, and draw conclusions. Some examples of their listening skill include:

• paraphrasing information learned during presentations;

• following multi-step directions on an assigned task;

• critiquing research presentations by peers based on information learned during earlier class discussions;

• concentrating on a small group discussion despite noises in the classroom;

• making accurate inferences about characters based on listening to an audiotaped story.

Fifth Grade

1 Listens to acquire information and understanding.

Fifth graders are learning to listen with a critical ear. They can begin to judge the accuracy of information, form opinions, and make decisions based on prior knowledge. Relevant reflection and thoughtful questioning based on what they hear can be expected. Examples of their listening skills include:

• listening to three different classmates describe methods of solving a math problem and then comparing and evaluating the methods;

• synthesizing into note form the main ideas of an oral presentation (a peer's research report, a visiting speaker's talk, a video presentation);

• analyzing information presented orally;

• listening to and then analyzing musical performances.

II Language and Literacy

II Language and Literacy

A Listening continued

Kindergarten

2 Follows directions that involve a series of actions.

Children often forget instructions or become distracted before they have completed a series of actions. The ability to focus and remember is important for the development of logical thinking, allowing the child to connect ideas and reach conclusions. Children demonstrate these skills by:

• following a set of instructions without reminders (for example, following the preparatory steps needed for going outside);

• leaving the classroom earlier than other children to deliver a message to the school secretary, and then meeting the class at the door to the playground;

• remembering instructions given earlier (for example, remembering to go to the circle area after snack today rather than to the usual quiet reading area);

• retelling a set of instructions to a classmate.

First Grade

2 Follows directions that involve a series of actions.

Six year olds are developing the ability to listen carefully to directions that have been spoken, interpret their meaning, and carry them out. They often forget or become distracted before they have completed a set of instructions. Examples of how children demonstrate their increasing skill in following directions include:

• listening to someone give a series of related instructions and following them without reminders;

• helping a classmate who didn't hear or understand the directions by carefully repeating them;

• hearing a peer explain a game's directions and then playing it correctly.

Second Grade

2 Follows directions that involve a multi-step sequence of actions.

Second graders can understand and follow multi-step directions and they will usually ask questions if unsure about what to do. Second graders demonstrate this by:

• listening to a series of related directions for a science activity, and following them;

• repeating the directions for a homework assignment to a classmate who was out of the room when it was assigned;

• teaching a peer how to play a game shortly after having heard how to play it.

Third Grade

2 Follows directions that involve a multi-step sequence of actions.

By the time children are in third grade, they can listen to multi-step directions, review them in their mind, and then carry them out. They are likely to ask specific questions if unsure about what to do. Examples of how third graders demonstrate this ability include:

• listening to someone give a set of multi-step directions for using a computer program and then following them;

• relaying directions for an assignment that was given when a classmate was absent;

• completing a survey and graphing project that involves a complex set of directions.

Fourth Grade

No equivalent performance indicator at this level.

Fifth Grade

No equivalent performance indicator at this level.

II Language and Literacy

B Speaking

Kindergarten

1 Speaks clearly, conveying ideas in discussions and conversations.

Although clear articulation may still be a challenge for some five year olds, their speech should be clear and understandable most of the time. (This indicator also may be assessed by observing the children's use of alternative communication systems, such as gesture, sign, or communication boards.) Many kindergartners have not had extensive opportunity for exploratory conversations, nor experience in answering questions with more than single words or short phrases. Children show emergent skills in this area by:

• retelling the morning events in more than short phrases;

• relating a story in sequence;

• asking questions in sentence form rather than with a few words;

• participating in conversations in interactive ways;

• relaying a message from the teacher to the school secretary.

First Grade

1 Speaks easily, conveying ideas in discussions and conversations.

When offered opportunities for exploratory conversation and discussion, six year olds are able to use increasingly detailed language to convey meaning about ideas and information. Some ways six year olds demonstrate the ability to speak easily include:

• using appropriate words to express pleasure, sadness, anger, or frustration to peers and adults in ways that make their feelings apparent;

• contributing relevant ideas to a discussion;

• offering explanations about what is happening in the classroom such as, how and why a building is being constructed in the block corner.

Second Grade

1 Speaks easily, conveying ideas in discussions and conversations.

Language is important to the social life of seven year olds. They can begin to describe events and ideas with an increasing number of details. These children progress from simple to more complex sentences in their spoken language. Examples of this include:

• making relevant contributions to class discussions;

• using descriptive language to express ideas, opinions, and feelings when conversing with others;

• using language to explain problem-solving strategies (for example, explaining how 24 cookies were shared evenly by five children).

II Language and Literacy

Third Grade

1 Speaks easily, conveying ideas in discussions and conversations.

For eight year olds, the ability to speak easily includes speaking clearly, varying tone and volume appropriately, and using an increasingly descriptive vocabulary. Examples of how an eight year old speaks easily include:

• using precise language to express ideas, opinions, and feelings in group discussions;

• telling a story, or presenting an oral report to a small group or the entire class, looking at the audience and using pauses and gestures appropriately;

• using language to explain how a problem was solved (for example, describing the steps they followed to double a recipe for cookies).

Fourth Grade

1 Speaks coherently, conveying ideas in discussions and conversations.

Most nine year olds are comfortable sharing their thoughts with another individual or in small groups. When presented with ongoing opportunities to engage in discussions and conversations, children become more willing to speak in larger classroom groups. They use complete sentences most of the time and begin to speak in more complex sentences. Examples include:

• making relevant contributions to class discussions by expressing ideas, opinions, and feelings;

• incorporating new vocabulary into discussions (using new words learned from a thematic unit);

• delivering short, planned and rehearsed oral presentations;

• telling a story to a small group of students.

Fifth Grade

1 Conveys ideas confidently and coherently.

Most ten year olds feel comfortable enough in their language skills to participate in a variety of social and academic situations. They are becoming more adept at retrieving and utilizing vocabulary in appropriate context. Examples include:

• making relevant contributions to class discussions by using clear, concise language to express ideas, opinions, and feelings;

• incorporating new vocabulary into spoken expression (using new words learned from a thematic study);

• speaking with ease in a variety of situations (greeting parents and guests at a school function, developing a media presentation on a theme for a selected audience, giving an oral presentation, reading orally);

• participating in public events that require spontaneous reactions or planned speaking (debates, panel discussions, interviews).

II Language and Literacy

B Speaking continued

Kindergarten

2 Uses language for a variety of purposes.

Five year olds are often fascinated with words and how they sound (for example, rhyming, making up new words, trying out jokes, or making up puns). This interest is apparent in the following examples:

• making up lists of rhyming words, including invented words;

• trying out new vocabulary words in sentences;

• telling a joke to a friend or making up new jokes (such as Knock-Knock jokes);

• asking questions relevant to an event reported by another child;

• explaining the use of cultural expressions to classmates.

First Grade

2 Uses language for a variety of purposes.

Six year olds are becoming increasingly comfortable using language to convey emotions, ideas, and information, as well as to ask questions and express humor. Examples of how six year olds use language include:

• trying new vocabulary while telling or writing a story;

• describing what was observed in a science experiment;

• using expressive language in dramatizations or when telling a story;

• making up a rhyming game or a new verse to a song.

Second Grade

2 Uses language for a variety of purposes.

Children in second grade begin to recognize that language is used differently in different contexts (for example, how one speaks in a group versus in informal conversations). They can begin to use language to inform, persuade, give directions, entertain, and express personal opinions and feelings. They are learning to differentiate between making comments and posing questions. Examples of ways they use language include:

• using colorful and imaginative language as a way to enhance descriptions;

• expressing humor by telling jokes and riddles, and making plays on words;

• using expressive language to tell stories, narrate skits, or dramatize scenes;

• asking a clarifying question after listening to a classmate's story.

Third Grade

2 Uses language flexibly for a variety of purposes.

Third graders recognize that language is used differently in different contexts (for example, how one speaks in a group versus in informal conversations). They have increasing ability to use language to inform, persuade, give directions, entertain, and express personal opinions and feelings. They are increasingly able to differentiate between making comments and posing questions. Examples of ways they use language include:

• making a thoughtful comment after listening to a classmate's story;

• engaging in debates and offering persuasive arguments;

• using language to express humor (puns, riddles, jokes);

• using expressive language in skits and plays.

Fourth Grade

2 Uses language flexibly for a variety of purposes.

Fourth graders use language to convey emotions, ideas, and information. As students actively engage in different kinds of language experiences (explaining strategies used to solve math problems or making predictions about scientific investigations) they become more confident and versatile in their ability to use language. Examples of how they use language include:

• using new vocabulary words in context across the curriculum to discuss and explain ideas (to describe responses to paintings, solutions to math problems, or scientific investigations);

• participating in debates or panel discussions and offering persuasive points of view;

• using language dramatically to act out roles in simulation plays or skits;

• learning words in another language to better communicate with a friend.

Fifth Grade

2 Uses language flexibly for a variety of purposes.

Fifth graders experiment with language and find increasingly sophisticated ways of using it. They may invent new words or create languages so that they can talk in "code." They will often argue a point enthusiastically, especially with an audience (even if they do not necessarily believe they are right). Examples include:

• engaging in debates or panel discussions and offering persuasive points of view;

• using language expressively to act out a role in a simulation, play, or skit;

• expressing feelings and opinions effectively (in a literature study group, as a response to a controversial subject);

• learning words in another language to communicate with a peer or an adult who speaks that language.

II Language and Literacy

C Literature and reading

Kindergarten

1 Listens with interest to stories read aloud.

Interest is a key factor in children's listening ability. They can often sit for long periods of time listening to a "good" story, but will squirm and fidget if made to sit still and attend to something that does not capture their interest. Examples of their developing skill in this area include:

• joining group storytime with anticipation and pleasure;

• understanding a story that has been read to the group and then discussing the meaning of actions in the story (for example, giving a possible explanation for why Chicken Little thought the sky was falling);

• requesting that favorite stories be read at storytime or during choicetime;

• going to the listening center to hear a story on tape.

First Grade

1 Listens with interest to stories and other text read aloud.

Interest in listening to stories read aloud is key to the six year old's developing skills as a reader. Through exposure to books and stories, children begin to learn reading skills and concepts (front cover, title, left to right, top to bottom, page to page, predicting what comes next, using pictures to make predictions). Examples of how six year olds demonstrate their interest include:

• making comments on text read aloud during discussion periods;

• asking to look at a book after it has been read aloud;

• looking for other books by the same author in the class library;

• relating personal experiences to those depicted in the text.

Second Grade

No equivalent performance indicator at this level.

Third Grade

No equivalent performance indicator at this level.

Fourth Grade

No equivalent performance indicator at this level.

Fifth Grade

No equivalent performance indicator at this level.

Kindergarten

2 Shows independent interest in reading-related activities.

As children become familiar with books, they independently begin to explore the wealth of information and pleasure that books provide. This interest and exploration is essential to learning how to read. Children show a growing interest in books by:

• looking at books during choice time;

• pretending to read a book using pictures or memory as clues;

• listening to a story on tape while following along in the accompanying book;

• looking to books for information about road-building machinery or to find the name of a particular dinosaur;

• asking for new and different books to be read aloud.

First Grade

2 Shows independent interest in reading-related activities.

As six year olds develop as readers, they are likely to be excited about and eager to practice their emerging skills in reading activities ("big book" stories, listening center, letter and card games). They independently explore the many pleasurable and informational qualities of books. This interest is crucial to their becoming competent readers. Examples of how they demonstrate this interest include:

• sitting with another child looking at or reading books;

• participating in group oral reading experiences ("big book" stories, daily messages, poems, songs);

• playing a reading-related game with interest;

• listening to a taped story and following along with the accompanying text;

• trying to interpret stories, messages, signs, and other forms of print in the environment;

• reading familiar books over and over.

Second Grade

1 Shows sustained interest in independent reading activities.

As children make the transition from early readers to more fluent or independent readers, they demonstrate interest in, appreciation for, and positive attitudes towards reading activities (stories read aloud, independent reading, listening center, word games). Some ways second graders show these interests are:

• reading for pleasure and relaxation;

• choosing to spend time listening to books at the listening center;

• looking for books related to a personal interest (books about baseball, horses, or dinosaurs);

• listening with interest and concentration to stories read or signed to them;

• finishing a book and then wanting to read another by the same author.

Third Grade

1 Shows sustained interest in a variety of independent reading activities.

As third graders become more independent and fluent readers, their interests and attitudes about reading can be examined apart from their actual reading abilities. Examples of how third graders show interest in literature and reading include:

• reading several books by the same author;

• selecting books based on a personal interest;

• making connections between personal experiences and literature;

• incorporating ideas from a story they heard into their own writing;

• sharing, reviewing, and recommending books to others.

Fourth Grade

1 Reads fluently and independently.

Nine year olds begin the transition from learning how to read to reading for information. Their new fluency allows them to explore more diverse reading materials (for example, poems, short stories, novels, journals, nonfiction, newspapers, magazines, plays) and to seek information in ways that were not previously possible. Fourth graders can read from several different sources to research topics, to pursue a particular interest, or for enjoyment. Examples include:

• reading a variety of materials in a sustained manner;

• using informational books for reference purposes (for example, to find out about early Aztec architecture);

• voluntarily selecting reading materials or activities that reflect pleasure and personal interest (author, subject matter, or genre);

• participating with interest in literature study groups.

Fifth Grade

1 Reads fluently and independently.

By fifth grade, most students read fluently. Their versatile and independent reading habits allow them to explore increasingly diverse reading materials (for example, poems, plays, newspapers, magazines, novels, journals, non-fiction). They can be expected to read from different sources to research topics, pursue interests, or for enjoyment. Examples of how fifth graders read fluently and independently include:

• choosing and sustaining interest in books for pleasure and information;

• using informational books for reference purposes (to find out about medieval culture, or the invention of airplanes);

• using a software manual well enough to play a computer game;

• participating with interest in literature study groups.

II Language and Literacy

C Literature and reading continued

Kindergarten	First Grade	Second Grade

Kindergarten

3 Predicts what will happen next using pictures and content for guides.

As children become more involved with the content of stories, they often want to put their own thoughts and ideas into the text. Five year olds show involvement in the reading process by:

• looking at pictures and guessing what will happen next;

• predicting what will happen to characters in a story based on their actions thus far;

• looking at the picture on the cover of a book and guessing what the book is about;

• guessing book or story content or plot from the book's title.

First Grade

3 Uses strategies to construct meaning from print.

To become readers, children must understand that reading involves constructing meaning from text. To do this requires using a variety of strategies in an integrated way. Strategies include: making predictions from the pictures and text; using graphophonic (letter-sound), semantic (context), syntactic (structural) cues; relying on prior knowledge; and skipping difficult words and then re-reading. Beginning readers are likely to use just a few of these strategies. Examples include:

• making predictions about how to read a word based on pictures on the page;

• using graphophonic relationships and pictures to figure out unfamiliar words in books or on signs and other print vehicles;

• accurately guessing an unfamiliar word by using the context and letter-sound recognition (for example, knowing the story is about insects, looking at a picture, knowing the "m" sound and guessing "mosquito" correctly).

Second Grade

2 Uses a variety of strategies to construct meaning from print.

To become readers, children must understand that reading involves constructing meaning from text. To do this requires using a variety of strategies in an integrated way. Strategies include: making predictions from the pictures and text; using graphophonic (letter-sound), semantic (context), syntactic (structural) cues; relying on prior knowledge; and skipping difficult words and then re-reading. As second graders become more fluent readers, their repertoire of strategies increases. Examples of how they use strategies include:

• guessing an unfamiliar word accurately by using both pictures and initial consonants;

• making a prediction about the text based on prior knowledge;

• self-correcting after looking at a picture and realizing that although the misread word made sense in the sentence, it wasn't accurate;

• skipping a difficult sentence while reading and then later going back to figure out what was missed.

Third Grade

2 Uses a wide variety of strategies to construct meaning from print.

Competent readers understand that reading involves constructing meaning from text. To do this requires using a variety of strategies in an integrated way. Strategies include: making predictions from the pictures and text; using graphophonic (letter-sound), semantic (context), syntactic (structural) cues; relying on prior knowledge; and skipping difficult words and then re-reading. By third grade, children should be using a wide variety of strategies to read fluently. Examples of how they use these strategies include:

• skipping words that are not familiar and not important to the meaning of the story;

• using prior knowledge about a subject to help with recognition of difficult words;

• using graphophonic cues to sound out difficult words;

• self-correcting when reading silently or aloud.

Fourth Grade

2 Uses a variety of strategies to gain meaning from text.

Nine year olds become more fluent readers as they use a combination of strategies to comprehend text (structural analysis, predictions, phonetic cues, context clues, prior knowledge). They can begin to apply appropriate strategies to different content areas (using context and prior knowledge to read science and social studies materials). Examples of how students use strategies to construct meaning include:

• using contextual clues to interpret a newspaper article;

• attempting to sound out challenging and unfamiliar words using phonetic cues;

• self-correcting errors when reading aloud;

• relying on prior knowledge to interpret difficult text.

Fifth Grade

2 Chooses appropriate strategies to construct meaning from text.

As fifth graders become more fluent in their reading, they automatically select and apply appropriate strategies (structural analysis, prediction, phonetic cues, context clues, and prior knowledge) as they read familiar and unfamiliar texts. They understand that different texts demand different strategies and this understanding helps them understand more complex material. Examples of how students use strategies include:

• extending the use of structural analysis skills and their understanding of phonics to decode complex words;

• using contextual clues and peer discussions to comprehend difficult text;

• using a combination of previewing techniques when choosing new books; (chapter titles, "blurb" on the outside of book, information about the author);

• figuring out approximate meaning and continuing to read even though every word is not understood;

• interpreting character behavior and plot development in order to anticipate story events.

II Language and Literacy

C Literature and reading continued

Kindergarten

4 Retells information from a story.

An important pre-reading skill is the ability to retell a story in sequence and to show an understanding of what has been read aloud. Ways children show they can recall what has been read to them include:

• retelling a story in sequence;

• participating with other children in a puppet show that dramatizes a story recently read to them;

• participating in a play about a story;

• recalling the main events in a story;

• discussing why a book ended as it did;

• thinking about the intent of a character in a story (for example, why Horton sat on the egg).

First Grade

4 Understands and interprets a story or other text.

When first graders recall a part of a story they have heard or read, relate a story to their own experience, or notice something about a story (a pattern, a rhyme, the way the pictures tell the story), they show that they are making sense of text. Examples of how first graders demonstrate these skills include:

• remembering and describing an event that happened in a story;

• retelling a short story just read or heard;

• reflecting about why a story ended as it did;

• asking a question about why something happened in a story;

• dramatizing part of a story.

Second Grade

3 Understands and interprets a story or other text.

Second graders demonstrate understanding of what they have read by recalling story details, relating a story to personal experience, and suggesting an interpretation of the events or characters in the story. Examples of how second graders respond to text include:

• describing a particular story character in a book report or a reading journal, or during group discussion;

• posing a question about why a particular story event occurred as it did;

• dramatizing a scene from a story;

• creating an interpretive painting or sculpture based on a story;

• writing a sequel to a story.

Third Grade

3 Understands and interprets stories or other texts.

Opportunities to respond to stories through discussions, writing, dramatization or using other art media enable children to synthesize, interpret, and make personal connections to what they read. Responding to increasingly complex text requires children to organize their thinking. They do this by identifying the main idea, important characters, central action, and setting. Examples of how third graders demonstrate textual comprehension include:

• describing a story event, character, setting, or structure during group discussion;

• depicting scenes from a story using a variety of artistic media (drama, painting, poetry, songs);

• reflecting on a character's actions by relating them to personal experience;

• writing about or discussing how a story might end.

Fourth Grade

3 Analyzes and interprets information from a story or other text.

As nine year olds read and discuss stories and other texts, they begin to identify central ideas, recognize the author's point of view, and analyze characters' motives and personality traits. Their response to what they read (through writing, discussion, dramatization, art work) shows their understanding of the text and expresses the personal meaning they bring to and find in the text. Ways that fourth graders demonstrate textual comprehension include:

• recalling important information about a text;

• depicting characters or scenes from a story using a variety of artistic media (dramatizing, painting, writing a poem or a song that captures a mood or a feeling);

• using a combination of previewing techniques when choosing new books (book title, "blurb" on the outside of the book, information about the author);

• describing in some detail an event, a character, or the setting in a story;

• predicting or anticipating character behavior and plot development.

Fifth Grade

3 Analyzes and interprets information from various texts.

As ten year olds read and discuss text, they can identify central ideas and the author's point of view, and analyze characters' motives and personality traits. Their response to what they read (through writing, discussion, artwork, and dramatization) shows their understanding of the text and expresses the personal meaning they brought to and found in the text. Examples include:

• using the author's language in recounting significant story events;

• describing with some detail a story event, character, or setting, and expressing its relevance to the story;

• comparing and contrasting different literary styles;

• recognizing the structure of a story and being able to compare it to that of other stories (mystery, adventure, drama, fable, short story, science fiction);

• listening critically during a book discussion and expressing a contrary opinion supported by specific evidence from the text.

II Language and Literacy

II Language and Literacy

C Literature and reading continued

Kindergarten	First Grade	Second Grade
5 Recognizes the association between spoken and written words.	**No equivalent performance indicator at this level.**	**No equivalent performance indicator at this level.**

Early reading skills include the understanding that written symbols represent specific words that are always the same (the "Exit" sign over the door, or labels on objects in the classroom). The child begins to understand that these words are used to convey specific messages, thoughts, and ideas. Children exhibit this awareness by:

• picking out their names on classroom lists and beginning to recognize their friends' names;

• beginning to recognize familiar words on the cover of a favorite book;

• developing a personal list of words recognized on sight;

• asking about the various signs used in the classroom (the "Exit" sign, or the word "fish" on the fish tank);

• beginning to recognize key words and symbols on the computer when playing games.

Third Grade

No equivalent performance indicator at this level.

Fourth Grade

No equivalent performance indicator at this level.

Fifth Grade

No equivalent performance indicator at this level.

❚ Language and Literacy

C Literature and reading continued

Kindergarten	First Grade	Second Grade
No equivalent performance indicator at this level.	No equivalent performance indicator at this level.	4 Reads text independently for varied purposes.

Second Grade

Second graders can begin to apply their knowledge and strategies to read purposefully and for extended periods of time. They recognize that they can read for pleasure and to gain information. Examples of how second graders demonstrate the ability to read for a variety of purposes include:

• reading for pleasure at school and at home;

• using reference books (dictionaries, encyclopedias);

• finding library books independently that relate to personal interests or class topics;

• getting to know an author's work by finishing one book and then immediately reading another by the same author.

Third Grade

4 **Reads text fluently, independently, and for varied purposes.**

Third graders can apply their knowledge and strategies to read fluently, purposefully, and for extended periods of time. They recognize that they can read for pleasure and to gain information. Examples of how third graders demonstrate the ability to read for a variety of purposes include:

• reading for pleasure at school and at home;

• using reference books (dictionaries, encyclopedias);

• reading non-fiction books to learn more about topics of personal interest;

• enjoying a particular genre of literature (mysteries, adventures, biographies).

Fourth Grade

4 **Locates and uses a variety of texts to gain information.**

As fourth graders begin researching topics, they become more familiar with the purpose of different texts and their formats; for example, dictionaries and encyclopedias are understood as having two distinct purposes. Though nine year olds are gaining familiarity with several ways to use reference materials, they often need the guidance of adults to help them use these resources effectively. Examples of how a student might use reference materials include:

• referring to encyclopedias to find basic facts or subject overviews;

• identifying various sources of information that might have helpful information (nonfiction books, magazines, maps);

• using a dictionary to learn the meaning of unfamiliar words read in books;

• using card catalogues or computers to locate library books;

• using informational books for reference purposes (nonfiction, dictionaries, encyclopedias).

Fifth Grade

4 **Locates and uses a variety of texts to gain information.**

Most fifth graders have had experience using a card catalog or a computer to search for information. Ten year olds can be expected to seek information from different kinds of references and audiovisual materials and by talking with subject specialists. Some ten year olds continue to need adult guidance to help them organize tasks and use their resources effectively. Examples include:

• locating information from a variety of sources (almanacs, maps, atlases, field guides);

• using a table of contents and index to determine if a book contains needed information;

• using informational books for reference purposes;

• using a card catalogue or computer to find books about a topic and then locating the books in the library.

II Language and Literacy
D Writing

Kindergarten

1 Uses letter-like shapes or letters to depict words or ideas.

As children begin to understand that writing communicates their thoughts to someone else, they become invested in being able to produce words, even if they do not possess conventional writing and spelling skills. Children this age enjoy:

• recognizing the letters on a keyboard;

• reading back the story written in their journal, even if the writing symbols and spelling are unique to the child;

• experimenting with written symbols by making marks that resemble letters to capture an idea;

• entering their own name or other words on the computer;

• writing familiar words, sometimes asking for help in forming the letters or spelling the words.

First Grade

1 Writes words, phrases, and sentences to convey meaning.

For many six year olds, the process of writing is an act of the moment; there is very little sense of writing for a specific audience. The pleasure in the process is usually connected to something else, such as producing a drawing, making a sign, or creating a list. Examples of how six year olds write for a variety of purposes include:

• telling or writing about a picture, drawing, or painting;

• making lists and signs for projects and activities throughout the classroom;

• writing a caption to accompany a science observation of the monarch butterfly;

• writing a note to the teacher or a friend.

Second Grade

1 Uses writing to convey meaning for a variety of purposes.

Second grade children can begin to understand that writing is a way to communicate ideas and organize information. Examples of how second graders write for a variety of purposes include:

• writing poetry, how-to books, or plays;

• writing a story about a personal experience;

• writing down information collected during a survey;

• writing about a math problem in a math journal;

• writing captions or descriptive sentences to accompany a science observation.

Third Grade

1 Uses writing to convey meaning for a wide variety of purposes.

By third grade, children can recognize writing as a way to communicate ideas and organize information. Examples of how they write for a variety of purposes include:

• writing stories, poetry, or a play in journals and writing folders;

• taking research notes and then composing a report;

• recording information for a graph;

• writing a letter to a friend;

• writing about math problems in a math journal.

Fourth Grade

1 Uses different forms of writing to communicate.

By fourth grade, students should be aware of the many purposes that writing serves across the curriculum (narrative, investigative, informative, interpretive, argumentative). Fourth graders explore different genres, including story writing, research writing, and poetry to describe curricular experiences. They begin to demonstrate a personal writing style. Examples of how students write for a variety of purposes include:

• creating vivid and colorful poetry;

• writing fiction and nonfiction stories;

• using writing across the curriculum (to describe solutions to math problems, write about science observations, take notes during interviews or videos);

• writing detailed research reports;

• writing letters (to pen pals, to an organizations for information, to thank class guests);

• writing a play.

Fifth Grade

1 Uses different forms of writing to communicate.

Fifth graders write throughout the school day for many different purposes (for example, narrative, informative, investigative, interpretive, argumentative). Their creative and expository writing reflects an increased awareness of the audience for whom they are writing. They use writing as a way to analyze, synthesize, and interpret information across the curriculum. Examples include:

• writing poetry, stories, plays, letters, journal entries, narratives, and prose for self-expression;

• taking notes (during interviews, or while viewing videos or listening to presentations);

• using writing across the curriculum (to describe solutions to math problems, or science observations);

• writing a letter to someone (governor, state senator, congressman) stating an idea or concern;

• using different moods and tones to enhance personal expression;

• taking risks as a writer (trying new genres, introducing stories in new ways, trying different voices).

▣ Language and Literacy
D Writing continued

Kindergarten	First Grade	Second Grade

Kindergarten

2 Copies or writes words needed for work or play.

Children begin to understand the power of written words when they see that messages, such as "Please Leave Standing" on a sign in front of a block structure, have an impact. Children show that they understand the power of written words by:

• copying words to convey messages (for example, "Stop" or "Go");

• recognizing that putting their names on a product signifies that it was done by them;

• realizing that a caption created for a picture or painting can tell a story about the drawing;

• copying a note to take home;

• making a sign, such as "Hospital" or "Shoe Store," for the dramatic play area;

• copying labels from around the room;

• using the keyboard to write their name or a personal message.

First Grade

No equivalent performance indicator at this level.

Second Grade

No equivalent performance indicator at this level.

Third Grade

No equivalent performance indicator at this level.

Fourth Grade

No equivalent performance indicator at this level.

Fifth Grade

No equivalent performance indicator at this level.

❚ Language and Literacy

D Writing continued

Kindergarten	First Grade	Second Grade
No equivalent performance indicator at this level.	**2 Recognizes conventions of print.**	**2 Recognizes and uses some print conventions;**

First Grade

For the six year old, being able to recognize conventions of writing includes: using a left-to-right writing pattern; spacing between words; recognizing the difference between upper and lower case letters; and having a beginning sense of sentence form. Examples of how first graders demonstrate recognition of these conventions include:

• noticing punctuation in text during a shared reading lesson with a "big book";

• spacing between all words when writing in a journal;

• using both upper and lower case letters (with some accuracy) when writing.

Second Grade

For second graders, being able to recognize conventions of writing includes: using upper and lower case letters correctly; having a sense of sentence form; using capitals at the beginning of sentences and a period or other form of punctuation at the end. Examples of how second graders demonstrate their increasing ability to recognize and use conventions include:

• using upper and lower case letters correctly;

• noticing forms of punctuation when reading text and attempting to apply them to their writing;

• experimenting with the function of other forms of punctuation besides periods, such as question marks, exclamation points, and quotation marks;

• reviewing a rough draft and identifying a few mechanical errors (for example, omitted capitals, periods, or words).

Third Grade

2 Uses conventions of written language with increasing accuracy.

Many third graders know the basic conventions of writing (for example, use of capitals, periods, and question marks). However, what they know and what they actually use in everyday writing often differs substantially. They demonstrate increasing understanding of how to use these conventions by:

• using capitalization correctly (for example, capitalizing the first word in a sentence, the pronoun "I", and names of people);

• reviewing text with a friend and identifying where sentences end;

• attempting to use punctuation to clarify written work (question marks, quotation marks, commas);

• using some conventions accurately when writing final or neat drafts.

Fourth Grade

2 Uses the conventions of written language with increasing accuracy.

Nine year olds often demonstrate their recognition of basic writing conventions (capitals, ending punctuation and internal punctuation) during conferences with peers in which they provide feedback. They need encouragement to proofread their work and apply conventions of grammar. Evidence of their ability to write using the conventions of language include:

• applying correct syntax and usage in first-draft writing (word order, tense, subject/verb agreement);

• using capitalization correctly (for the first word in a sentence, the pronoun "I," and proper nouns);

• using punctuation correctly (end marks, commas, apostrophes, quotation marks);

• correcting their own writing more independently;

• seeking and responding to corrective feedback.

Fifth Grade

2 Uses the conventions of written language with increasing accuracy.

Fifth graders are continuing to refine basic writing skills. They can use the conventions of writing (syntax, punctuation, and forming paragraphs) to improve the clarity of their written communication. They can often provide constructive feedback to their peers that indicates that they know more than they can actually apply to their own writing. Evidence of this understanding includes:

• using correct syntax and usage in writing (word order, tense, subject/verb agreement);

• using end marks, commas, apostrophes, and quotation marks correctly;

• self-correcting more independently;

• seeking and responding to corrective feedback.

Kindergarten	First Grade	Second Grade
No equivalent performance indicator at this level.	**3 Generates ideas for simple stories and composes drafts.**	**3 Composes stories with a beginning sense of sequence.**

Kindergarten

No equivalent performance indicator at this level.

First Grade

3 Generates ideas for simple stories and composes drafts.

As first graders become writers, they develop the concept that a story consists of characters and action. They rely on personal experiences for ideas, often drawing pictures to help them write. Frequently, more of their story is represented by the pictures than the words. Examples of how first graders demonstrate their emerging composition skills include:

• hearing a story read aloud and using it as the basis to write their own story;

• drawing a set of pictures based on a personal experience and then writing captions for the pictures;

• making several "books" about a topic that together begin to comprise a sequenced story.

Second Grade

3 Composes stories with a beginning sense of sequence.

Seven year olds are beginning to write for an audience, although this often inhibits them. They frequently set out to tell "everything" in their stories and have difficulty staying with a main theme. Although their stories may be long, they make only minimal sequential sense. Examples of how they compose sequential stories include:

• making a story map of the entire sequence, even though the story they actually write doesn't follow the entire map;

• basing a story on a personal experience and providing the beginning, middle, and end;

• sequencing ideas in a very short story;

• recognizing that a story lacks an ending and asking classmates for help.

Third Grade

3 **Composes sequential stories with understanding of beginning, middle, and end.**

Eight year olds have a clearer awareness of their audience. By using a variety of strategies in the pre-writing stages, such as talking, writing a plan, or making a story map or web, third graders can begin to draft sequenced stories that have a clear beginning, middle, and end. Examples of how third graders demonstrate their ability to compose a sequential story include:

• drawing on varied strategies for planning a story (talking with a friend, recalling a personal experience, considering another author's style), and then beginning to write;

• recognizing that a story is going on too long, stopping, and asking for ideas on how to create an interesting ending;

• using a favorite author's style to help organize a story.

Fourth Grade

3 **Writes in an organized and coherent manner.**

Most nine year olds can recognize that a piece of writing has logical order (introduction, body, conclusion). By using various strategies in the prewriting stages, such as talking, collaborating, outlining, and rehearsing, nine year olds can learn to organize their thoughts and shape their writing as they work on their first drafts. They can develop an idea by providing supporting details. Children show their composition skills by:

• including detail in ways that enrich stories;

• organizing ideas from beginning to end with a logical progression;

• relying on imitation of an author's style to help structure and organize their writing;

• writing paragraphs with main ideas, supporting sentences, and concluding sentences.

Fifth Grade

3 **Writes in an organized and coherent manner.**

Fifth graders can be expected to write paragraphs with main ideas, supporting sentences, and concluding sentences. Their writing across the curriculum shows an understanding that all writing should have a logical sequence and organization. They are learning to include abstract ideas, and experiment with style and form while maintaining a coherent story structure. Examples of their skills of composition include:

• using a variety of strategies for rehearsing or planning stories and then beginning to write (talking with friends, recalling personal experiences, considering another author's style);

• emulating a favorite author's style;

• organizing ideas from beginning to end with a logical progression;

• planning a particular style and/or structure for a story, and following through (beginning the story at mid-point, leaving the reader in suspense in anticipation of a sequel, writing in the first person).

II Language and Literacy

D Writing continued

Kindergarten	First Grade	Second Grade

Kindergarten

No equivalent performance indicator at this level.

First Grade

4 **Makes a change in the content of a story for clarity or elaboration.**

When given some encouragement to read their own writing, six year olds may realize they have left out an important detail. When they add this to their story, they are beginning to engage in the revision process, which is different from editing. Revision addresses content and editing focuses on mechanics. Examples of emerging revision skills include:

• re-reading a story, deciding there is a missing detail and adding it;

• attaching a new page to a completed story to add another section;

• returning to a story after a day or two and adding something new to it.

Second Grade

4 **Rereads writing and makes changes to clarify or elaborate.**

When given an opportunity to reread and share their writing, seven year olds may decide they have left out an important detail or included too many. They may decide to change some words to make the text more interesting or descriptive. The modification or change in content is revision, as compared with editing which addresses mechanics. Some ways second graders demonstrate revision skills include:

• re-reading a story, deciding there is a missing detail and adding it;

• sharing a story with a friend or the class and deciding to change or add to it;

• returning to a story after a day or two and adding something new to it.

Third Grade

4 Rereads and reflects on writing, making changes to clarify or elaborate;

When given an opportunity to reread and share their writing, eight year olds may decide they have left out important details or included too many. They can be encouraged to add more descriptive language, or rewrite sentences to create greater clarity. Some ways third graders demonstrate revision skills include:

• reading a story to a peer and talking over whether to add or remove some information;

• sharing a story with the class and deciding to change the beginning or ending;

• after writing for a while, deciding that a topic is too broad and narrowing it down;

• working on a story over time (for example, for several days) and making changes along the way.

Fourth Grade

4 Rereads, reflects, and makes revisions.

Revision is challenging for nine year olds who may enjoy writing drafts of stories but are not sure how to revise them. Their beginning revision skills include refining a story for clarity, sequence, and organization. Examples of revision skills include:

• deciding if ideas flow from one paragraph to another;

• deciding that a topic is too broad and narrowing it to something more specific;

• writing a new beginning to strengthen the story and capture the reader's interest;

• rewriting a confused or repetitive section.

Fifth Grade

4 Rereads, reflects, and makes revisions.

Revision continues to be a challenging step in the writing process for fifth graders. However, when they have ongoing opportunities to read and listen to their classmates' writing and to share their own, they can be expected to anticipate questions that a teacher or a peer might ask about their writing and then include those revisions more spontaneously. Examples include:

• deciding if a paragraph has a main idea and supporting details;

• reading the draft to a friend and listening to how it sounds, and reworking an unclear section;

• refining introductions and conclusions;

• rearranging and reorganizing a piece into a more cohesive form.

II Language and Literacy

II Language and Literacy

D Writing continued

Kindergarten

No equivalent performance indicator at this level.

First Grade

No equivalent performance indicator at this level.

Second Grade

No equivalent performance indicator at this level.

Third Grade

5 Reviews a rough draft and makes some mechanical corrections.

After third graders have finished composing, they can review rough drafts and make some spelling, capitalization, sentence structure, and punctuation corrections. Examples of skills in this area include:

• re-reading a story and adding omitted words;

• re-reading a story composed on a word processor and making corrections;

• reading a story aloud to note where pauses are, and then putting in missing periods;

• deciding that all of the sentences begin the same way and rearranging some phrases;

• working with a partner to read a story and recognizing the need for editing.

Fourth Grade

5 Proofreads a rough draft and makes corrections in its mechanics.

After fourth graders have finished composing, they can be expected to review rough drafts and make some corrections (without the aid of the teacher) in spelling, capitalization, sentence structure, and punctuation. Examples of developing proofreading skills include:

• re-reading and noting omitted and inserted words;

• using a word processor to proofread and revise;

• checking for spelling and punctuation mistakes.

Fifth Grade

5 Proofreads a rough draft and makes corrections in its mechanics.

Ten year olds are ready to initiate the proofreading process independently. They can make corrections in punctuation, capitalization, spelling, and sentence structure using various resources as guides. Examples include:

• re-reading a story and omitting run-ons and sentence fragments;

• looking over a story independently or with a friend and correcting misspelled words;

• reading stories aloud to note where the pauses are and putting in missing punctuation;

• using a word processor to draft, revise, and assist with proofreading.

II Language and Literacy

▮ Language and Literacy

D Writing continued

Kindergarten

No equivalent performance indicator at this level.

First Grade

No equivalent performance indicator at this level.

Second Grade

No equivalent performance indicator at this level.

Third Grade

No equivalent performance indicator at this level.

Fourth Grade

6 **Shows increasing control of standard spellings.**

Fourth grade students make the transition from invented spelling to standardized spelling and now start to apply more formalized rules. Examples include:

• using a dictionary or computerized spell checker as a reference tool;

• figuring out how to spell a word by relating it to similar, previously learned words;

• recognizing structural patterns (forming plurals, identifying past and present verb forms, adding suffixes);

• noticing misspelled words and making corrections when reviewing drafts;

• applying spelling rules and skills across the curriculum.

Fifth Grade

6 **Shows control of standard spellings.**

By fifth grade, most students have mastered basic sight words and primarily use conventional spelling. They can apply rules to various groups of words (adding "s", "es", or "ies" to create plurals), and recognize and use patterns (sound patterns as in consonant blends, visual patterns as in *ough*, and semantic patterns as in using the suffix *scope*). Examples of these skills include:

• applying spelling rules and skills to writing across the curriculum;

• figuring out how to spell a word by relating it to previously learned, similar words;

• noticing misspelled words and making corrections when reviewing drafts;

• including irregular words in their spelling repertoire;

• using a computer spell check or dictionary to find out how to spell words.

II Language and Literacy

▐▐ Language and Literacy

D Writing continued

Kindergarten

No equivalent performance indicator at this level.

First Grade

No equivalent performance indicator at this level.

Second Grade

No equivalent performance indicator at this level.

Third Grade

No equivalent performance indicator at this level.

Fourth Grade

7 Shows beginning understanding of research writing.

The fascination of nine year olds with the natural and physical world motivates them to seek out information to pursue specific interests. As they gather information, they can use writing as a means to express and share their findings. Examples of developing research-writing skills include:

• choosing a form of note-taking that is meaningful (webbing, pyramid, note-cards);

• sorting and organizing information (determining in what order information should be written);

• outlining a subject area through main ideas (researching a culture: customs, climate, clothing, food, homes, resources);

• reflecting on main ideas and insights about a topic through writing or discussions;

• using the writing process to organize research into a coherent presentation.

Fifth Grade

7 Demonstrates research-writing skills.

As ten year olds become more independent in their learning, they are increasingly able to pursue their own interests and more complex assignments given by teachers. Fifth graders are beginning to learn a more formalized approach to research, which requires developing the skills of note taking, outlining, and creating drafts. Examples of these skills include:

• choosing a form of note taking that is meaningful (webbing, notecards, pyramid);

• using a variety of formats to express ideas and information (tables, charts, maps);

• conducting surveys or interviews and writing up the findings;

• outlining a subject area through main ideas, subtopics, and detail;

• connecting new information to previously acquired information;

• reflecting on main ideas and insights about the topic through writing or discussions;

• using the writing process to organize research into a coherent presentation.

II Language and Literacy
E Spelling

Kindergarten	First Grade	Second Grade
No equivalent performance indicator at this level.	**1 Uses strategies to create invented spellings.**	**1 Uses varied strategies to create invented spellings.**

First Grade

1 Uses strategies to create invented spellings.

Early writers construct spellings first with initial sounds, then initial and ending sounds, gradually using a letter for each sound in the word. Examples of how first graders demonstrate their ability to use strategies to create invented spellings include:

• using initial consonants and letter-sound correspondence to spell, and saying sounds and words aloud when writing;

• using resources from their environment (peers, personal dictionaries, charts, books) to help with invented spelling;

• using letter names to represent sounds ("r" for are or "u" for you).

Second Grade

1 Uses varied strategies to create invented spellings.

Developing writers continue to use invented spellings as a way of writing more fluently. Examples of how children create invented spellings include:

• making use of resources in the environment to support invented spelling (peers, personal dictionaries, charts, books);

• sounding out words while writing to identify the different sounds that make up words;

• recalling familiar words and creating close facsimiles of their spellings.

Third Grade

No equivalent performance indicator at this level.

Fourth Grade

No equivalent performance indicator at this level.

Fifth Grade

No equivalent performance indicator at this level.

II Language and Literacy

E Spelling continued

Kindergarten	First Grade	Second Grade
No equivalent performance indicator at this level.	**2 Attempts to use closer approximations of conventional spellings.**	**2 Uses some conventional spellings.**

First Grade

2 Attempts to use closer approximations of conventional spellings.

When children have extensive opportunities to use writing purposefully in the classroom, they begin to approximate conventional spellings more closely. For first graders this includes: using letters for every sound, putting a vowel into every syllable, or only missing one letter of the word. Some ways that first graders demonstrate this are:

• recognizing the difference between invented spellings and conventional spellings in their own writing;

• copying conventional spellings when making signs, lists, or labels;

• using conventional spellings of words they often see in print.

Second Grade

2 Uses some conventional spellings.

When children have extensive opportunities to use writing purposefully in the classroom, they begin to approximate conventional spellings more closely. Examples of how second graders demonstrate their ability to use conventional spelling include:

• using conventional spellings of words they often see in the classroom when writing in a journal;

• noting incorrect inventions and spontaneously correcting them when re-reading drafts;

• using correct spellings of words related to classroom topics.

Third Grade

1 Uses standard spellings with some frequency.

By third grade, children should begin to use standard spellings with some frequency. This includes spelling common word prefixes and endings correctly, and recognizing and using patterns of spelling (such as double letters and vowel combinations). Third graders demonstrate their ability to use standard spellings by:

• using standard spelling when writing drafts;

• noticing misspelled words and making corrections when reviewing drafts;

• using standard spellings in daily assignments (homework, math problems, science observations).

Fourth Grade

No equivalent performance indicator at this level.

Fifth Grade

No equivalent performance indicator at this level.

II Language and Literacy

Mathematical Thinking

The focus in this domain is on children's approach to mathematical thinking and problem-solving. Emphasis is placed on how students acquire and use strategies to perceive, understand, and act on mathematical problems. Mathematics is about patterns and relationships, and about seeking multiple solutions to problems. In this domain, the content of mathematics (concepts and procedures) is stressed, but within the larger context of understanding and application (knowing and doing).

III Mathematical Thinking

A Approach to mathematical thinking

Kindergarten

1 Shows interest in solving mathematical problems.

Mathematical thinking involves sequential thinking using given information to derive a conclusion, and asking questions and applying strategies to find answers. Five year olds are ready to learn about problems that need solutions and to develop simple problem-solving strategies. They show this emerging skill as they play and interact by:

• asking questions to clarify problems (for example, "Will the new rabbit cage be big enough for all the baby bunnies?");

• solving problems by guessing and checking, using concrete objects (such as figuring out how many apples are needed for snack if each child is served half an apple);

• informally estimating whether there are enough blocks to build a road from here to there, and then testing the guess by building the road;

• playing computer games that involve problem-solving or elementary mathematical concepts.

First Grade

1 Uses strategies to solve mathematical problems.

To solve mathematical problems, first graders begin to use a variety of strategies (including trial and error, noticing patterns, making drawings or diagrams, using mental math, counting on, counting backwards, or counting in groups). Some ways they demonstrate the ability to use strategies are:

• using trial and error (for example, figuring out how many pattern blocks or tangrams fit into a closed shape);

• determining the number of wheels on six bicycles by making a drawing;

• counting by five using tally marks when determining how many people want apple or orange juice for snack.

Second Grade

1 Uses strategies to solve mathematical problems.

Second graders begin to use systematic approaches to problem solving, enlisting a variety of strategies (including trial and error, noticing patterns, making drawings or diagrams, using mental math, using a calculator, counting on, counting backwards, or counting in groups). Second graders demonstrate this skill by:

• counting checkers by two to determine the winner of the game;

• making drawings to figure out the solution to a problem (for example, how many legs on three horses and four chickens);

• using a calculator and a calendar to determine the days in a year after estimating the answer;

• counting backwards (for example, beginning with a set of 20 cubes, removing one and saying 19, removing another and saying 18, etc.).

Third Grade

1 Uses strategies to solve mathematical problems.

Third graders can use systematic approaches and strategies for problem solving (including trial and error, guessing and checking, making drawings, diagrams or charts, using mental math, using a calculator, counting on, counting backwards, or counting in groups). Third graders demonstrate this skill by:

• using trial and error to figure out how many unifix cubes it will take to balance a scale;

• making a drawing to figure out different ways to combine members of the class into even teams;

• making a chart or table (for example, to keep track of how many times a six is rolled in 30 rolls of a die);

• mentally calculating the score in Scrabble, counting by tens and then adding the ones;

• checking an estimate by using a calculator.

Fourth Grade

1 Uses strategies flexibly to solve mathematical problems.

Nine year olds use logical thinking to select the appropriate strategies needed to solve problems. Their repertoire of strategies can include making charts, lists, or tables, and using guess and check, or trial and error. They should be familiar with ways to use drawings, models, and diagrams to solve mathematical problems. Examples of strategies that fourth graders might use are:

• using trial and error (for example, to find two numbers whose sum is 43 and whose difference is 9);

• creating a table and using a pattern to solve problems involving meters and kilometers (if you walk 1 km in 10 minutes, how many km will you walk in one hour? in two hours? in three hours?);

• applying a mathematical strategy to solve problems that arise in other subject areas (determining how much soil is needed for a planting project);

• using a calculator to solve problems involving large numbers.

Fifth Grade

1 Approaches mathematical problems with curiosity and flexibility.

Fifth graders can be expected to understand a problem, choose a strategy, follow their plan, and then evaluate their success. They can recognize that there may be several ways to solve a problem and express similar ideas. They can choose the best plan from a variety of strategies (making reasonable estimates, working problems backwards, making drawings or diagrams, looking for patterns, creating systematic lists) for solving a problem. Some ways fifth graders demonstrate this skill include:

• continuing to work on a problem that might take a few days to solve;

• identifying a problem and considering ways to solve it (for example, figuring out the surface area of the skin on their body);

• choosing and applying mental, manual and/or calculator processes to various problems (determining how many words are in a book after first estimating the number);

• creating a chart to determine prime and composite numbers.

III Mathematical Thinking

A Approach to mathematical thinking continued

Kindergarten

2 Uses words to describe mathematical ideas.

When teachers ask children to describe how they know the number of crackers needed at the snack table, or how they assembled a puzzle, or why they built a block structure with a particular design, they are encouraging children to attach language to mathematical and geometric thinking. Children verbalize their thinking by:

• explaining that they chose a puzzle piece because its shape matched the other shape;

• telling a friend or teacher that they have just built the tallest block structure in the school;

• explaining that they put all the long sticks in one box and all the short sticks in another box;

• using a variety of quantity words as they play at various interest areas;

• asking at the sand table for a bigger container because they want to mold a larger building or move more sand.

First Grade

2 Describes and explains mathematical thinking through drawings and words.

Discussion, representation, reading, and writing are essential to learning mathematics. With encouragement, six year olds can use words and pictures to describe and explain how they solve problems. Expressing their reasoning methods helps them to clarify their ideas and to attach language to mathematical thinking. Some ways they do this include:

• sorting a group of objects, and then explaining, "I sorted these things by how flat or round they are — flat ones in this group, round ones in the other group";

• explaining the strategy used to assemble a puzzle;

• showing several peers how and why ramps were constructed on a block building;

• describing quantities in terms of "more," "not as much," or "about the same."

Second Grade

2 Describes and explains mathematical thinking through drawings and words.

Discussion, representation, reading, and writing are essential to learning mathematics. When given opportunities to use words and pictures to explain their reasoning, seven year olds clarify their ideas and learn the language attached to mathematics. Some ways they do this include:

• describing the strategy used to estimate the number of buttons in a jar, and then detailing how the actual answer was derived;

• teaching a peer their method of solving a problem (explaining, for instance, that she counts by tens as a way of determining how many M&Ms are in a jar);

• explaining a pattern in the class weather chart;

• using ordinal numbers to describe objects or events by their position (for example, first, third).

Third Grade

2 Communicates mathematical thinking through oral and written language.

Discussion, representation, reading, and writing are essential to learning mathematics. Math journals and logs, and class discussions help third graders express their thinking and reasoning about mathematical problems. They can be expected to use various oral, written, pictorial, and graphical methods. Examples of how third graders communicate mathematical thinking include:

• participating in math discussions (for example, describing solutions to math puzzles and games);

• explaining why a weight estimate of a pumpkin is logical;

• drawing a picture to show how the class will evenly share two pizzas;

• using mathematical terms in oral and written descriptions.

Fourth Grade

2 Communicates mathematical thinking using oral or written language.

Nine year olds should be able to express their mathematical thinking by using graphs, tables, charts, diagrams, speech, and written prose. Examples of mathematical communications include:

• discussing mathematical ideas;

• writing in a math journal about the strategies used to solve problems and explaining why solutions are reasonable;

• describing how strategies can be applied to other mathematical problems;

• drawing a picture to explain a mathematical idea to a younger child.

Fifth Grade

2 Communicates mathematical thinking using oral and written language.

Ten year olds can use reading, listening, and observing skills to interpret new mathematical ideas. They reveal mathematical thinking by using oral, written, pictorial, and graphical methods. Examples include:

• paraphrasing a problem;

• synthesizing and summarizing a group's strategy for solving a problem;

• using a math journal to write about the problem-solving process (what strategies worked best, why decisions were made along the way);

• creating a diagram, table, graph, model, or chart to describe mathematical data;

• using appropriate mathematical language and notation.

III Mathematical Thinking

▥ Mathematical Thinking

B Patterns and relationships

Kindergarten	First Grade	Second Grade

Kindergarten

1 **Recognizes patterns and duplicates or extends them.**

Children acquire mathematical thinking skills while playing or working with concrete objects. Working with abstract numbers on sheets of paper like those in workbook pages, does not give children an intrinsic understanding of quantity, mass, and relationships. Children gain this understanding by using and interacting with real objects. They begin to understand patterns (part of the foundation of mathematical thinking) by:

• seeing the pattern in a string of beads and determining which bead is needed to continue the pattern;

• duplicating a pattern of clapping (for example, two fast claps and a pause, then two slow claps and a pause);

• recognizing a sequence on a computer game;

• creating patterns with a variety of materials, such as Legos, pattern blocks, Cuisenaire rods, and describing the pattern;

• experimenting with patterns using markers or finger paint.

First Grade

1 **Makes, copies, and extends patterns with actions, objects, and words.**

By six, children can create and extend patterns concretely and pictorially, and then describe them. They can also begin to recognize patterns in numbers and the environment. Examples of this include:

• making, copying, and extending a pattern with voice, body, and musical instruments;

• identifying the rule needed to extend a pattern or determine a missing element in a pattern (for example, jump, hop, hop, ___, hop, hop);

• creating a pattern with pattern blocks or other manipulative materials;

• drawing a pattern with crayons and describing it;

• recognizing patterns on objects in the classroom (for example, the grid on the radiator or the tiles on the floor).

Second Grade

1 **Makes, copies, and extends patterns with actions, objects, words, and numbers.**

The more familiar children are with patterns, the more readily they begin to notice them in a variety of formats (for example, visually and auditorially, concretely and pictorially, with numbers and in nature, linearly and in a matrix). By seven, children should also recognize patterns in numbers (even and odd numbers). Some ways seven year olds demonstrate their patterning skills include:

• creating many different representations of the same pattern (for example, first with pattern blocks, then with cut out representations, and finally as a drawing);

• identifying the rule needed to extend a pattern or determine a missing element in a pattern (15, 13, 11, ___, 7, 5);

• recognizing patterns in calendars or daily schedules;

• discovering patterns in games (such as winning moves in tic tac toe).

Third Grade

1 Uses the concept of patterning to make predictions and draw conclusions.

For eight year olds, work with patterns includes creating, extending, and describing patterns with actions, objects, and numbers. By this age, children should be applying their understanding of patterns to make predictions, draw conclusions, and solve problems (for example, adding or subtracting a constant number to or from a series of numbers, noticing the pattern, and predicting the next number). Some ways third graders demonstrate their patterning skills include:

• creating an intricate drawing of a pattern on paper and reproducing it with another material (for example, drawing a pattern on paper and reproducing it as a weaving);

• identifying the rule needed to extend a pattern or determine a missing element in a pattern (for example, 109, 99, 89, 79, …);

• finding the dates for all the Tuesdays in a given year;

• determining how many yellow hexagons would be needed to complete the entire design, given one row of a pattern block design.

Fourth Grade

1 Uses the concept of patterning to make predictions and draw conclusions.

Fourth graders can be expected to look spontaneously for patterns and relationships as a strategy for analyzing and solving problems related to number, geometry, and measurement. By anticipating such questions as "What do you think comes next?" or "What do you notice about your patterns?" nine year olds can generate their own predictions and conclusions. Examples include:

• generalizing and verbalizing number patterns to make predictions and draw conclusions;

• completing or creating one-step function tables (e.g., $n-6$ = ___ or $3n$ = ___);

• using patterns to predict multiples (knowing the multiples of 12 by adding multiples of 10 to multiples of 2; $12 \times 4 = 10 \times 4 + 2 \times 4$);

• identifying a pattern in a sequence of whole numbers, extending the sequence, and proposing a rule to describe the relationship;

• using patterns across the curriculum to make predictions (spelling patterns, artistic patterns on primitive pottery, human settlement patterns).

Fifth Grade

1 Applies an understanding of patterns to make predictions and draw conclusions.

By fifth grade, children should understand patterns and relationships abstractly, including the concepts of functions and equations, proportion and ratio, and probability. Ten year olds can be expected spontaneously to detect patterns and communicate rules underlying patterns in a systematic and organized way across the curriculum and use them to make logical predictions. Examples include:

• identifying patterns and functions by adding, multiplying, subtracting, or dividing two constant numbers (multiplying 1, 2, 3, 4 by 7, then subtracting 2 from each result and finding the totals to be 5, 12, 19, and 26);

• using constants on a calculator to make predictions;

• determining how to make a three-dimensional figure from a design;

• using the Fibonacci pattern to determine numbers in patterns;

• using patterns to create designs (tessellations).

▐▐▐ Mathematical Thinking

B Patterns and relationships continued

Kindergarten	First Grade	Second Grade
2 Sorts objects into subgroups, classifying and comparing according to a rule.	**2 Sorts, classifies, and compares objects, recognizing attributes of subgroups.**	**2 Sorts, classifies, and compares objects using attributes and quantities.**

Kindergarten

Sorting objects into groups according to attributes is difficult for some children at this age. Many five year olds can only perceive one attribute at a time; they are not able to integrate several attributes, such as sorting by color and size. Alternatively, they may know that animals are four-footed and furry but they cannot divide them into subgroups of wild animals and farm animals. Examples of skills in sorting and comparing include:

• sorting all the pegs or counting bears into groups by color;

• sorting through a box of buttons and making up their own rules of organization (for example, these are all rough and these are all smooth, or these have two holes and these have four holes);

• stating a "rule" about the way objects have been sorted;

• noticing that these pattern blocks have six sides and are yellow, and these blocks have three sides and are red.

First Grade

For six year olds, this skill encompasses sorting objects and describing the sorting rule, sorting by a given attribute, and comparing objects for similarities and differences. At this age, children can begin to compare one quantity to another to determine if they are equal or if one is more or less than another. They can also order objects by size. Ways children demonstrate their sorting skills include:

• sorting a collection of keys into two groups: keys with ridges on one side and keys with ridges on both sides;

• describing similarities and differences in the shapes and sizes of seeds;

• comparing a collection of objects and putting them in order by size (for example, small to large, long to short);

• using sorting and classifying in social studies or science activities (organizing a list of neighborhood stores into two groups, ones with counters and no tables, and ones with tables and chairs).

Second Grade

Seven year olds can sort objects and describe the rule, sort by a given attribute, and compare objects for similarities and differences. They can compare quantities to determine if they are equal or if one is more or less than another as well as begin to order groups using the names of ordinal numbers. At this age children may notice the overlap of sets. Ways children demonstrate sorting skills include:

• sorting math materials by several attributes (for example, making a group of large plastic shapes and a group of small wooden ones);

• creating a visual example of intersecting sets (for example, separating shoes into those with laces and those without, and observing that both groups have leather shoes);

• counting two sets of buttons to determine which contains more;

• using classifying and ordering in social studies or science activities (lining up a group of plant seedlings in order by size and labeling them accordingly).

Third Grade

2 Uses sorting and classifying to organize information and make predictions.

Sorting, classifying, and comparing objects and quantities requires logical thinking. By the time children are eight, they can create subgroups according to specific and multiple attributes. Eight year olds can also be expected to observe and create intersecting or overlapping sets. Examples of how children demonstrate their understanding of sorting, classifying, and comparing include:

• devising rules that describe a sorting system with two or three attributes;

• ordering objects by their weight;

• noticing similarities and differences within one type of shape (for example, that all triangles have three sides but do not have the same size angles);

• using sorting and classifying in social studies or science activities (grouping photographs of animals into two groups, those with backbones and those without).

Fourth Grade

2 Uses sorting, classifying, and comparing to analyze data.

Sorting, classifying, and comparing objects requires logical thinking. Fourth graders can go beyond the most concrete observations and start devising rules that describe a sorting system with as many as four attributes. Examples of their skills include:

• identifying two intersecting sets by creating a Venn diagram (comparing the human body to a machine);

• making charts that depict ratios ($1 buys 2 tickets, $2 buys 4 tickets, $3 buys 6 tickets);

• creating subgroups according to specific attributes.

Fifth Grade

2 Uses sorting, classifying, and comparing to analyze data.

Ten year olds can be expected to examine a collection of information and logically place their data in related groups, organizing facts according to a rule. They demonstrate their understanding of sorting, classifying, and comparing data by:

• determining if it is possible to make a figure using four triangles that has five, six, seven, or eight sides;

• creating subgroups according to specific attributes (breaking down birds of prey into buteos, accipitors, or falcons);

• creating a Venn diagram (exports from Chile and Peru);

• comparing two quantities to determine a ratio (miles per gallon for different cars).

III Mathematical Thinking

III Mathematical Thinking

B Patterns and relationships continued

Kindergarten	First Grade	Second Grade
3 Orders or seriates a variety of objects on the basis of several attributes.	**No equivalent performance indicator at this level.**	**No equivalent performance indicator at this level.**

Groupings and comparisons based on a single attribute that changes systematically (small to large, short to long, soft to loud) are called seriation. It is a precursor to later exploration of number, quantity, and mathematical relationships. Seriation is based on defining differences, while classification is based on sorting by similarities. Five year olds start by being able to order only four or five objects, and gradually increase to eight or 10. Some examples of seriating include:

• arranging four rods from shortest to longest;

• making a collage of leaves, starting with the smallest, smoothest, or brightest;

• making a display of several stones, arranged from the smallest to the largest;

• arranging objects in any of the classroom interest areas into a planned progression.

Third Grade

No equivalent performance indicator at this level.

Fourth Grade

No equivalent performance indicator at this level.

Fifth Grade

No equivalent performance indicator at this level.

▥ Mathematical Thinking
C Number concept and operations

Kindergarten	First Grade	Second Grade
1 Shows understanding of the concept of number and quantity.	**1 Shows understanding of quantity.**	**1 Models, reads, writes, and compares whole numbers.**

Kindergarten

1 Shows understanding of the concept of number and quantity.

Five year olds are usually able to count accurately by rote to 10 or 20. However, many children are not yet able to use one-to-one correspondence (pointing to and assigning a number to each object in a group). Even after children are able to count with one-to-one correspondence, they may not associate counting with the number of objects in the group or with quantity in general. Evidence of an understanding of number and quantity includes:

• explaining that there are nine people in the circle today, after counting them;

• putting out enough carpet squares for the six children who will be sitting there during storytime;

• announcing that they brought in eight stones from the playground;

• using number words to show understanding of the common numerical property among five children, five cups, five trucks, and five blocks;

• using a calendar to count the number of days until a class trip.

First Grade

1 Shows understanding of quantity.

Six year olds show their comprehension of whole numbers when they can model numbers using objects and use one-to-one correspondence when counting. It is essential that the child understand number meaning rather than simply number-naming or rote counting. This means knowing that a number can be represented in many ways (for example, 10, ten, two sets of five stars, etc.). Examples of how six year olds demonstrate this understanding include:

• pointing to each object in a group as they count them (for example, shoes, children, boxes on a graph);

• linking number symbols to concrete materials (building 30 cubes to match the numeral 30);

• reading and writing numerals purposefully (recording the score in a game, writing the numbers on a calendar).

Second Grade

1 Models, reads, writes, and compares whole numbers.

Seven year olds show their comprehension of whole numbers when they model, order, and compare two-digit numbers using objects. Very often children can count to high numbers but have little understanding of what the numbers mean. In second grade, children who understand the meaning of quantity can more readily progress to working with higher numbers. Seven year olds demonstrate their understanding of numbers by:

• using both numbers and numerals to identify quantities (count 25 objects and use the numeral 25 or the word twenty-five to label it);

• counting to 100 or more (for example, when keeping track of how many days of school have passed);

• reading and writing numerals purposefully, such as recording card game scores;

• recognizing that 30 is the same quantity if it is 30 horses or 30 M&Ms or 15+15 red dots;

• describing the comparative relationship of numbers (20 is smaller than 50).

Third Grade

1 Models, reads, writes, and compares whole numbers.

Eight year olds can often calculate addition and subtraction algorithms without comprehending the meaning of two- and three-digit whole numbers. Evidence of true understanding of whole numbers is seen when children compare and order numbers by relative size (120 comes before 210 because it is smaller). Examples of understanding of whole numbers include:

• using numbers to identify quantities (for example, in scoring games, handling money, estimating amounts);

• reading and writing numerals easily (in scoring games, calculating measurements, locating page numbers in an index);

• making reasonable estimates of quantities in the hundreds (such as saying there are three or four hundred days in a year).

Fourth Grade

1 Shows understanding of number quantities and their relationships.

By fourth grade, children should demonstrate understanding of number meanings and the relationships among numbers. This includes explaining place value using models and expanded notation. Examples include:

• explaining their reasoning when adding or subtracting two-, three-, and four-digit numbers using manipulatives;

• reading, writing, and comparing numbers up to 999,999, and applying them to real life situations;

• using mental computation strategies;

• estimating to the nearest 10, 100, 1000;

• recognizing the relative magnitude of number (7,201 is greater than 7,021).

Fifth Grade

1 Shows understanding of number quantities and their relationships.

Ten year olds show greater flexibility in their work with integers, fractions, decimals, and percents. They can be expected to measure physical objects and more complex phenomena accurately, and represent numbers in expanded notation to identify the place value of any digit in numbers up to one billion. Examples include:

• reading, writing and comparing numbers up to 999,999,999 and applying them to real life situations;

• mentally adding two-digit numbers to two- and three-digit numbers;

• estimating to the nearest 10, 100, 1000;

• explaining their reasoning when adding or subtracting two-, three- and four-digit numbers with manipulatives.

III Mathematical Thinking

III Mathematical Thinking

C Number concept and operations continued

Kindergarten	First Grade	Second Grade

Kindergarten

2 Begins to understand relationships between quantities.

As children gain mastery over the use of numbers and how numbers apply to quantity, they begin to explore the relationships of various quantities to one another. They become intrigued with the constancy of numbers (five is always five) but also begin to learn that numbers can represent fluid situations when things are taken away or added. Evidence of their understanding of quantity includes:

• counting two groups of blocks, and indicating which group has more and which has less;

• recognizing that five large objects are the same in terms of number as a group of five small objects;

• explaining that a group of four objects is now smaller because we took away two objects from the original group of six;

• explaining that quantity changes as things are added to or taken away from groups.

First Grade

2 Uses strategies to add and subtract one- and two-digit numbers.

First graders show competence with basic operations on numbers when they understand the processes of combining and separating groups. Familiarity with strategies for finding sums and differences with numbers up to 10 usually results in increased skill using operations on larger numbers. Strategies first graders are likely to use for combining and separating quantities include: counting on fingers, doubling (for example, 4+4, 5+5), and knowing "number families" (if 2+8 = 10, then 8+2 is also 10). Examples of how first graders use such strategies include:

• figuring out that 10–2 = 8 by holding up two hands and putting down both thumbs;

• determining one's score in a "go fish" game by adding doubles;

• figuring out sums in a dice game using doubles plus one (if 5+5 = 10, then 5+6 is one more than 10);

• counting a bunch of pennies by 2s.

Second Grade

2 Uses strategies to add and subtract numbers.

The more familiar second graders are with finding sums and differences with small numbers, the easier it will be for them to work with larger numbers. Games help children learn basic operational strategies. Second graders should be using strategies such as doubling (for example, 8+8, 6+6), doubling plus or minus one, knowing "number families" (if 2+8 = 10 then 8+2 is also 10), and knowing number facts. Examples include:

• calculating scores in card games using doubles and doubles plus one (for example, 6+7 = 13 because 7+7 = 14 and 6+7 is one less);

• relying on knowledge of number family relationships when figuring out a solution to a problem (if 9–3 = 6, then I'll have 60¢ left if I start with 90¢ and buy a 30¢ sticker);

• finding the difference between two scores in a game ("Your score was 25 and mine was 18, so you won by 7.");

• mentally calculating the value of a group of coins (two dimes and three nickels equals 35¢).

Third Grade

2 **Uses strategies to add and subtract numbers.**

Knowing strategies to find sums and differences with small numbers enables third graders to have flexibility and confidence when using operations on large numbers. Third graders can begin to apply what they know about numbers through 10 to multiples of 10. This includes using doubles, doubles plus and minus one, number families, and number facts up to 20. Games help children learn basic operational strategies. Examples of how they apply these strategies include:

• using a doubles strategy (4+4, 70+70) to calculate the cost of items from the school store;

• using number family relationships to solve a problem involving large numbers (if 5+7 = 12, then 50+70 = 120);

• mentally calculating the total weight of a group of objects (123 lbs. + 114 lbs. = 200+23+10+4, or 237 lbs.);

• counting in large groups (seeing three quarters and knowing they equal 75¢).

Fourth Grade

2 **Selects and uses appropriate strategies for addition and subtraction.**

By fourth grade, children are increasingly flexible in their use of strategies to find sums and differences. They can be expected to use estimation and mental computation to solve problems and to explain or demonstrate the relationship between addition and subtraction. Examples include:

• mentally adding two, two-digit numbers $(34+42 = (30+40) + (4+2) = (70+6) = 76)$;

• estimating approximate sums $(1,242+378 \approx 1,200+400$ or $1,600)$;

• estimating approximate differences $(358-211 \approx (300-200) + (60-10) = (100+50) = 150)$;

• using calculators to solve and verify solutions;

• using addition and subtraction algorithms appropriately in everyday problem-solving situations.

Fifth Grade

2 **Uses appropriate strategies for addition, subtraction, multiplication, and division.**

As fifth graders build their understanding of number concepts and operations by solving many different mathematical problems, they can be expected to explain the relationships between addition, subtraction, multiplication, and division. They are able to apply strategies that help them solve problems incorporating large numbers, use reasoning skills to analyze problems, determine what operations are best suited to solving them, and explain their thinking using various mathematical representations. Examples of this include:

• using diagrams to determine products or quotients (lattice multiplication or rectangular arrays);

• recognizing multiples in a 1–144 number chart and discussing patterns (why do 8 and 9 have more complex patterns than 7?);

• estimating approximate sums and differences $(23,456+878 \approx 23,000+1,000 = 24,000,$ or its inverse);

• estimating differences and using a calculator to verify solutions;

• estimating products and quotients.

III Mathematical Thinking

95

▥ Mathematical Thinking

C Number concept and operations continued

Kindergarten	First Grade	Second Grade
No equivalent performance indicator at this level.	**3 Begins to understand place value.**	**3 Shows developing understanding of place value.**

First Grade

Before children can grasp place value or regrouping, they must first understand two-digit numbers and groups of 10. Work with materials (Cuisenaire rods, Dienes blocks, trading games) helps children grasp the concept of grouping by tens. Examples of their beginning understanding of place value include:

• counting on from 10 (for example, given a group of 10 and asked to add three more objects, does the child count on from 10 or begin at one);

• recognizing the patterns of 10 on the calendar;

• building a tower of 10 unifix cubes and putting three more next to the tower to show 13, and saying "thirteen is the same as a group of ten plus a group of three."

Second Grade

Children must first have an understanding of grouping numbers into tens and ones before they can understand regrouping. Working with models to illustrate multi-digit numbers helps second graders learn the meaning of place value. Some ways second graders show their developing understanding of place value include:

• using a group of objects as a unit (for example, in a chip trading game);

• counting by 10 or in multiples of 10;

• calculating the value of a group of coins (two dimes and one nickel equals 25¢);

• describing or showing a two digit number in more than one way (with Cuisenaire rods, show 32 as three orange rods and two white rods, or 32 white, or two orange and 12 white).

Third Grade

3 Applies understanding of place value to problem solving.

Third graders understand place value when they build a model to illustrate a multi-digit number and when they can explain the expanded notation of a three-digit number. This understanding enables a third grader to explain the logic in regrouping problems. Some ways third graders demonstrate their understanding of place value include:

• explaining their reasoning while adding or subtracting two- and three-digit numbers in the context of a meaningful problem;

• mentally adding two, two-digit numbers by grouping the tens and ones and then combining to get a sum;

• writing the expanded notation of a number and explaining its meaning;

• calculating the value of a group of coins (six dimes, three nickels, and three pennies equals 78¢);

• representing a three-digit number in more than one way.

Fourth Grade

No equivalent performance indicator at this level.

Fifth Grade

No equivalent performance indicator at this level.

▥ Mathematical Thinking

C Number concept and operations continued

Kindergarten	First Grade	Second Grade
No equivalent performance indicator at this level.	**4 Makes reasonable estimates of quantities.**	**4 Makes reasonable estimates of quantities and checks answers.**

First Grade

Through estimation activities, first graders extend their understanding of number. They can begin to make realistic guesses using phrases such as same, almost, bigger than, and smaller than. Some examples of the ability to make reasonable estimates include:

• looking at a group of objects and deciding if it is more than 10, about 20, or less than 50;

• pointing to the approximate location of the number 45 on a multiples of 10 number line, and explaining why it is between 40 and 50;

• showing a beginning understanding of large numbers ("There are over a hundred children in the school.").

Second Grade

As second graders develop estimation skills, they come to understand that mathematics is not always about exactness. For second graders, understanding of estimation includes making realistic guesses using such phrases as near, about, close to, more than, greater than, and less than. By this age, children can check the reasonableness of their answers. Some examples of this include:

• looking at some objects and making a thoughtful guess about the amount that comes close to the actual amount (estimating that there are about 58 cubes in a jar that actually contains 50 cubes);

• showing an understanding of large numbers by estimating quantity (saying that about 75 children eat in the lunch room each day, or that there are more than 300 children in the school);

• looking at a collection of coins (nickels, dimes, and quarters), estimating total value, and then checking the guess on a calculator.

Third Grade

4 Makes reasonable estimates of quantities and checks answers.

As children learn to estimate, they come to understand that mathematics is not always about exactness. Their understanding of estimation includes making realistic guesses (for example, of quantities, time, money, measurements) and knowing how to check the reasonableness of answers. They can also begin to understand the concept of rounding numbers to multiples of 10. Some examples of this understanding include:

• estimating that there are about 300 cubes in a jar (that actually contains 350) and then counting to verify the estimate;

• using reasonable estimates when measuring (the bulletin board is about 2 yards long, the pumpkin weighs about 5 lbs., the Lego set costs about $5);

• knowing when to use an estimate as an appropriate solution to a problem ("We need about a hundred sheets of paper if everyone in the class needs four.").

Fourth Grade

3 Makes reasonable estimates of quantities and checks answers.

Nine year olds use estimation skills every day, particularly when working with time, food, or money. They can be expected to apply estimation strategies when solving problems involving measurement and quantity. Examples of their estimation skills include:

• determining when to use estimation as a strategy for solving problems of quantity (number of people who could fit in a stadium);

• rounding large numbers to get approximate answers;

• using estimation to determine time;

• using reasonable estimates when measuring (to create posters or artistic designs, to construct woodworking projects).

Fifth Grade

3 Makes reasonable estimates of quantities and checks answers.

Estimation is key to mathematical thinking. Ten year olds should know that estimation is sometimes the most effective strategy; not all problems require exact answers. They can estimate with fractions, decimals, and percentages. They can check the reasonableness of their solutions by computation and measurement. Examples of these skills include:

• using estimation to determine percent (e.g., figuring 40% of the profit made from fund-raising $349.07);

• using estimation to determine the reasonableness of an algorithm or a calculator result;

• estimating to find an approximate measurement (area, perimeter, capacity);

• using estimation skills with money (will $50 buy four pieces of clothing at $15.95, $7.95, $13.25, and $11.95?).

III Mathematical Thinking

III Mathematical Thinking

C Number concept and operations continued

Kindergarten

No equivalent performance indicator at this level.

First Grade

No equivalent performance indicator at this level.

Second Grade

5 **Uses simple strategies to multiply and divide.**

In second grade, children can be expected to explore multiplication and division in informal ways, such as creating pictures, using repeated addition, or solving division problems by sharing. Examples of how they demonstrate this include:

• creating a picture to show three rows of five in solving a problem about how to plant 15 plants in even rows);

• using repeated addition (7+7+7+7) to determine how many players are on four teams of seven players;

• dividing a deck of cards by giving each of four children in the game one card at a time, going around in a circle until all the cards are distributed, and then counting how many cards each person holds to solve the problem 52÷4;

• dividing objects into equal parts (cut an apple into four equal parts).

Third Grade

5 Uses some strategies to multiply and divide whole numbers.

Third graders can apply what they know about combining and separating groups of numbers (a group of five, three groups of five). By third grade, children can be expected to count in groups (2s, 3s, 5s), know some multiplication facts, and recognize patterns related to multiplication. Some examples include:

• seeing the relationship between repeated addition and multiplication ($7 \times 4 = 28 = 7+7+7+7$);

• counting in multiples to solve a practical problem (calculating how many cookies are in the six packages of four cookies each by counting by 4s);

• using manipulatives to determine products and quotients ("How many groups of four children will there be if our class of 28 divides up equally?");

• using number family relationships with multiplication and division and with multiples of ten (if $2 \times 9 = 18$, then $9 \times 2 = 18$, and $18 \div 2 = 9$; also $9 \times 2 = 18$, so $9 \times 20 = 180$).

Fourth Grade

4 Selects and uses appropriate strategies for multiplication and division.

Most fourth graders understand the relationship between division and multiplication. They are beginning to see that division means separating whole numbers into equal parts and that it is the inverse of multiplication. Children can be expected to demonstrate their knowledge that multiplying two factors yields a product and that a product divided by one of the factors equals the other factor. Experiences using manipulatives and drawings allow them to understand the meaning of division. Examples include:

• estimating quotients ($123 \div 4 \approx 120 \div 4$; $12 \div 4 = 3$; therefore $120 \div 4 = 30$);

• dividing sets by specific numbers (how many rows of 7 can be made with 42 tiles?);

• beginning to use mathematical language to convey ideas (dividends, divisors, quotients);

• solving problems using division.

Fifth Grade

No equivalent performance indicator at this level.

III Mathematical Thinking

III Mathematical Thinking

C Number concept and operations continued

Kindergarten

No equivalent performance indicator at this level.

First Grade

No equivalent performance indicator at this level.

Second Grade

No equivalent performance indicator at this level.

Third Grade

6 Shows some understanding of halves, thirds, and fourths as parts of wholes.

Use of concrete materials (pattern blocks, Cuisenaire rods, geoboards) helps children understand fractional relationships. Third graders can be expected to identify and interpret fractions as parts of wholes. They can explore fractions with objects and numbers. Examples of these skills include:

• dividing real objects into equal parts in a variety of ways and describing relative size (cuts an apple into four equal parts, two equal parts, eight equal parts and describes size differences);

• recognizing the relative values of ½, ⅓, ¼ (agrees that ½ of the pizza is more than ¼ and can show why);

• dividing sets into fractional parts (puts 24 M&Ms into three equal piles in order to find ⅓ of the total);

• combining and separating fractional parts (can assemble fraction puzzles showing that ½ + ¼ + ¼ = 1, and that 1− ¼ = ¾).

Fourth Grade

5 Shows beginning understanding of fractions, decimals, and percents.

As fourth graders study fractions, decimals, and percents more formally, they begin to demonstrate an understanding of order and equivalence. They continue to rely on models as they explore various ways to represent numbers. They can perform operations on fractions with common denominators. Decimals can be most readily understood using money. Examples of a fourth grader's understanding include:

• drawing the whole rectangle when only a fractional part is presented;

• using a ruler to determine measurements up to eighths;

• writing fractional numbers on a number line;

• estimating fractional numbers that apply to real world situations (estimating how much water is in the fish tank or identifying parts of an hour);

• doing addition and subtraction problems that involve sums of up to $1000;

• recognizing that $.10 is 1/10 of $1.00;

• reading and writing amounts of money in decimal form.

Fifth Grade

4 Shows an understanding of fractions, decimals, and percents.

Part/whole relations can be expressed in many different ways. Ten year olds recognize the need for ways to represent quantities other than whole numbers and understand the relationship among fractions, decimals, and percents. They can model, compute, and estimate using fractions, decimals, and percents and explain their thinking. Examples include:

• using models to relate fractions to decimals and to find equivalent fractions;

• estimating percentages of shaded squares;

• recognizing equivalent fractions using manipulative materials;

• using strategies to add, multiply, subtract, and divide fractions and decimals.

III Mathematical Thinking

III Mathematical Thinking

D Geometry and spatial relations

Kindergarten	First Grade	Second Grade

Kindergarten

1 Identifies, labels, and creates a variety of shapes.

As children play with unit blocks, table blocks, pattern blocks, shape sorters, peg boards, and geoboards, they gain a concrete understanding of shape and form. This concrete experience is important to later geometrical thinking and problem solving. As five year olds play and work in their environment, they gain a foundation in geometric constructs by:

• recognizing and creating circles, squares, rectangles, and triangles with varied materials (for example, crayons, a geoboard, folding paper);

• identifying objects of similar shape but different size;

• describing characteristics of shapes (for example, it has three sides, the sides are straight);

• identifying and labeling shapes found in the environment;

• drawing a variety of shapes and labeling them;

• using shape words to name unit blocks.

First Grade

1 Recognizes properties of shapes and relationships among shapes.

First graders are beginning to recognize and describe the properties of some shapes (for example, squares have straight lines and four sides). They can identify relationships between shapes (for example, there are two red trapezoids inside the yellow hexagon). By constructing and manipulating shapes (2-D and 3-D), they develop spatial thinking. Examples of how first graders demonstrate this understanding include:

• comparing, matching, and reproducing shapes (for example, with tangrams, geoboards, pattern blocks);

• recognizing the relationships between shapes (triangles and squares, or trapezoids and hexagons);

• recognizing specific properties of forms and shapes (number of sides, corners, faces);

• recognizing and naming the shapes in their environment.

Second Grade

1 Recognizes properties of shapes and relationships among shapes.

Second graders can be expected to recognize and describe the properties of several shapes. By exploring what happens when shapes are changed using manipulative materials (such as pattern blocks, tiles, and geoboards), they can discern relationships among shapes. Examples include:

• comparing and describing properties of shapes ("All triangles have three sides, some are tall and thin, others short and fat.");

• beginning to recognize parts of shapes and how shapes are constructed ("This rectangle has a pair of short lines, two long lines, and four angles.");

• beginning to recognize congruence (can copy exactly the size and shape of an irregular quadrilateral on a geoboard);

• using shapes and their names in everyday experience (observing them in nature, using them to sort and classify objects, creating designs that incorporate shapes).

Third Grade

1 Recognizes properties of 2-D and 3-D shapes and relationships among them.

Third graders can be expected to recognize and describe the properties of many polygons. They explore the relationships among shapes by adding to them, dividing them up, and noticing shapes inside other shapes using drawings and manipulatives (such as pattern blocks, tiles, geoboards). Examples of how children demonstrate this understanding include:

• recognizing the squares and triangles inside a polygon (using tangrams, geoboards);

• recognizing parts of shapes and how shapes are constructed (rectangles have two pairs of equal length sides and four right angles);

• using shapes and their names in everyday experience (observing them in nature, using them to sort and classify objects, creating designs that incorporate shapes);

• recognizing congruence (can copy exactly the size and shape of an irregular quadrilateral on a geoboard).

Fourth Grade

1 Identifies, classifies, and compares the properties of 2-D and 3-D shapes.

Fourth graders can be expected to recognize, describe, and compare two- and three-dimensional shapes. They manipulate, create, count, and measure one-dimensional properties of lines, two-dimensional properties of figures on a plane, or three-dimensional properties of objects in space. They can be expected to recognize congruent shapes using a systematic approach for identifying shape characteristics (for example, points, angles, sides). Examples of how children demonstrate this understanding include:

• investigating and predicting the results of combining, subdividing, and changing shapes;

• finding the area of simple two-dimensional shapes using models or diagrams;

• using tiles to represent area in square units;

• using cubes to represent volume in cubic units (construct a three-dimensional cubic structure based on a two-dimensional picture);

• solving multiplication problems by using graph paper or place value blocks (7×23 = 2 ten rods and 3 ones, 7 times).

Fifth Grade

1 Identifies, classifies, and compares 2-D and 3-D shapes.

Fifth graders are ready to explore more sophisticated spatial relationships. They continue to use concrete materials to explore geometrical relationships and can appropriately apply mathematical language such as congruent, equilateral, equiangular, obtuse, acute, oblique, regular, irregular, and symmetrical. They can compare, match, name, and reproduce three-dimensional shapes (for example, pyramid, cube, octahedron, icosahedron), and recognize parts of three-dimensional shapes and how they are constructed. Examples include:

• recognizing congruence (graphing pairs of congruent pyramids in a coordinate plane);

• comparing the areas and perimeters of shapes (different-sized triangles, squares, and rectangles);

• measuring the radius and diameter of various circles;

• creating platonic solids (square pyramid, hexagonal pyramid, dodecahedron).

III Mathematical Thinking

III Mathematical Thinking

D Geometry and spatial relations continued

Kindergarten	First Grade	Second Grade
2 Shows understanding of and uses positional words.	**No equivalent performance indicator at this level.**	**No equivalent performance indicator at this level.**

Children learn positional vocabulary and concepts as they understand and develop spatial awareness and a sense of symmetry and balance. The child learns these concepts best by discovery, experimentation, and such experiences as:

• placing an object inside and outside, behind and in front, under and above, beside and on a box on a table;

• understanding that this object (perhaps a chair) is nearer to me and farther from you;

• putting the blocks away beside the Little People;

• recognizing who is sitting beside the teacher and who is sitting in front of her;

• using positional words when playing in the dramatic play area or when building with blocks;

• using positional words spontaneously as they participate in play activities.

Third Grade

No equivalent performance indicator at this level.

Fourth Grade

No equivalent performance indicator at this level.

Fifth Grade

No equivalent performance indicator at this level.

III Mathematical Thinking

D Geometry and spatial relations continued

Kindergarten	First Grade	Second Grade

Kindergarten

No equivalent performance indicator at this level.

First Grade

2 **Explores and solves simple spatial problems using manipulatives and drawings.**

First graders reveal their developing sense of order, design, and spatial organization as they create drawings, build with blocks and Legos, and use math manipulatives (such as pattern blocks, tangrams, and geoboards). Examples of their developing spatial sense and ability to solve spatial problems include:

• making a ramp in a block building by using a series of triangular blocks instead of simply using a plank;

• creating a pattern block design using symmetry;

• drawing a picture of an apartment building or house that includes windows, chimneys, and doors, using balance and symmetry to make it realistic.

Second Grade

2 **Explores and solves spatial problems using manipulatives and drawings.**

For some children, a sense of order, design, and spatial organization comes naturally; for others it requires a great deal of careful planning. Work with math manipulatives (such as pattern blocks, tangrams, and geoboards) and drawings enables children to experiment with form and design. Second graders can be expected to explore symmetry and reflections (such as mirror images). Examples of their spatial sense and ability to solve spatial problems include:

• visualizing various solutions to spatial problems (for example, using pattern blocks, putting five diamonds or 10 triangles into the drawn outline of a flower);

• making a symmetrical design on a geoboard using only eight nails;

• creating reflection drawings (using the same four pattern blocks to construct the other side of a four-piece design);

• making a symmetrical design using LOGO or other graphics program on the computer.

Third Grade

2 Explores and solves complex spatial problems using manipulatives and drawings.

For some children, a sense of order, design, and spatial organization comes naturally; for others it requires a great deal of careful planning. Work with math manipulatives and drawings enables children to experiment with form and design. Third graders can be expected to explore symmetry, reflections (such as mirror images), and rotation. Examples of their spatial sense and ability to solve spatial problems include:

• visualizing various solutions to spatial problems (for example, using pattern blocks, putting five diamonds or 10 triangles into an outline of a flower);

• making a symmetrical design using only 16 pattern blocks;

• solving area problems (for example, filling a space using square color tiles in order to find out how many will cover the area);

• creating reflection drawings (using the same 10 pattern blocks to construct the other side of a 10-piece design);

• making a symmetrical design using LOGO or another graphics program on the computer.

Fourth Grade

2 Uses some strategies to solve problems involving spatial relationships.

By fourth grade, children can be expected to transform, combine, and divide geometric shapes. They can explore the relationship between geometric concepts and measurement. Examples include:

• planning various solutions to spatial problems (finding multiple ways to create a shape using Tangrams);

• solving problems that involve area and perimeter of polygons;

• constructing a design in LOGO on the computer using procedures and superprocedures in which different geometric shapes have been programmed;

• exploring tessellations, symmetry, and perspective;

• reading and drawing simple maps using coordinates.

Fifth Grade

2 Uses strategies to solve problems involving perimeter, area, and volume.

Fifth graders continue to build upon their sense of form, order. balance, and design to solve spatial problems using models to construct 2-D and 3-D shapes. They solve problems involving perimeter, area, and capacity. They can order and compare the relationships between perimeter and area of a given shape. Examples include:

• determining the perimeter of an area or shape (how much fence is needed to enclose a piece of land, or how much land is inside the fence);

• designing a graphics program (using LOGO on a computer with terms like SETX, SETY, XCOR, YCOR);

• predicting a pattern when plotting points on a grid;

• drawing and reading maps with coordinates.

III Mathematical Thinking

▥ Mathematical Thinking

E Measurement

Kindergarten	First Grade	Second Grade

Kindergarten

1 **Shows understanding of and uses comparative words.**

Five year olds are very interested in comparing sizes, shapes, and quantities of things (for example, "My truck is bigger than yours," or "You have more ice cream than I"). At five years of age, children are becoming more adept at using measurement to confirm their assumptions. Children show an understanding of measurement terms by:

• saying one child's bucket holds more sand than another's;

• noticing that one child is taller than another;

• recognizing that there are only a few cookies and that there are too many children for each to have one;

• using measurement words when building with blocks, at the sand table, or when exploring with Cuisenaire rods;

• using measurement words of comparison during the school day;

• noticing that the outside door is heavier than the classroom door.

First Grade

No equivalent performance indicator at this level.

Second Grade

No equivalent performance indicator at this level.

Third Grade

No equivalent performance indicator at this level.

Fourth Grade

No equivalent performance indicator at this level.

Fifth Grade

No equivalent performance indicator at this level.

▥ Mathematical Thinking

E Measurement continued

Kindergarten

2 Estimates and measures using non-standard units.

Children are adept at creating their own units of measurement when adults are receptive to their ideas. They are also fascinated with trying to see if their guesses or estimates are accurate. Examples include:

• guessing whether or not a container they have selected is big enough to hold all their marbles;

• estimating that a bird's nest weighs the same as five counting bears;

• stating that the road they just built is seven unit blocks long;

• using a common measuring stick to compare heights and lengths of objects.

First Grade

1 Describes, estimates and measures using non-standard units.

By exploring measurement with non-standard units, first graders begin to develop an understanding of the measuring process (such as counting and lining units up from a baseline) and the reasons for using consistent measuring units. Solving problems with various units (for example, unifix cubes, body parts, and books) helps children discover important measurement concepts. First graders can also be expected to estimate measurements using non-standard units. Some examples include:

• estimating length, height, or weight using non-standard measures (for example, hands, body lengths, and blocks) and then checking predictions;

• using non-standard units to determine length, weight, and volume (unifix cubes, one-inch cubes, Cuisenaire rods);

• comparing objects using a balance scale, and describing them as heavier or lighter.

Second Grade

1 Describes, estimates and measures using non-standard units.

Continued exploration of measurement with non-standard units enables second graders to develop their understanding of the measuring process as the counting of consistent measurement units. They can recognize some attributes of objects and events that can be measured (such as height, speed, weight, and area). They can be expected to estimate measurements and check predictions as well as solve problems involving measurement. Some examples include:

• estimating and comparing lengths, heights, and weights using non-standard measures (hands, body lengths, blocks) and then checking predictions;

• measuring with non-standard units to determine weight and volume (unifix cubes, one-inch cubes, Cuisenaire rods);

• comparing weights of objects using balance scales.

Third Grade

1 Describes, estimates and measures using non-standard and standard units.

By third grade, children can be expected to recognize the importance of consistent units of measure and solve measurement problems using non-standard and standard measures. Children should be familiar with the attributes of objects and events that can be measured (such as length, width, height, volume, and temperature) as well as measurement reference frames (such as about 1 ft., and 1 lb.). Third graders can explore area and perimeter using standard and non-standard measures. Some ways a child demonstrates understanding of measurement include:

• estimating standard measures, and then checking predictions;

• determining how much heavier, taller, or bigger one object is than another (for example, "The red magnet weighs 5 ounces more than the green one.");

• estimating the classroom perimeter and then measuring it with a trundle wheel.

Fourth Grade

1 Estimates and measures using standard and non-standard units.

Fourth graders continue to use standard and non-standard units to measure length, capacity, area, perimeter, weight, time, angle, and temperature. Children at this age should be able to make reasonable estimates for measurement problems and determine their accuracy through actual measurement. Some examples include:

• using LOGO computer commands to create angles;

• measuring height with a non-standard unit to create a ratio (for example, foot and forearm are about the same length: foot/forearm = 1/1);

• determining area and perimeter of polygons;

• creating historical timelines (creating a timeline relating to the history of American Indians);

• recognizing seasonal/time changes as they relate to natural phenomena (migration, hibernation, moon phases);

Fifth Grade

1 Describes, estimates, and measures using standard units.

Students should be able to estimate reasonably when figuring out problems. They use more precise measurements when calculating exact measures. They should be familiar with both customary and metric units. They have extended their understanding and vocabulary to include length, area, capacity, volume, mass, temperature, and time as ways to compare and quantify objects. Examples include:

• determining how many centimeter cubes can fit in a one-liter box;

• developing formulas to find the area of polygons;

• estimating length, area, angle, weight, mass, volume, capacity, or temperature, and checking predictions;

• constructing a woodworking project that requires accurate measurements (bird house, small chair, box with lid).

III Mathematical Thinking

III Mathematical Thinking

E Measurement continued

Kindergarten

3 Shows interest in common instruments for measuring.

Children are interested in the tools and instruments used by adults, although conventional measurement is usually not meaningful to them. Their interest in trying measurement tools to see how they work is demonstrated by:

• using a balance scale when comparing the weights of objects;

• incorporating measuring tools into their dramatic play (for example, "We need a cup of flour for these pancakes");

• using measuring cups at the water table to measure water, or tablespoons and teaspoons at the cooking table to add ingredients to the cookie recipe;

• using a ruler to measure the height of a plant;

• using classroom measurement tools (scales, rulers, cups) for activities such as cooking, building, and at the science table.

First Grade

2 Uses simple, common instruments for measuring.

Although first graders explore measurement problems using non-standard measures, they can begin to know the purpose of certain common measurement instruments (such as balance scales, thermometers, and rulers). Examples of children showing interest in and exploring the use of measurement instruments include:

• using a balance scale to compare the weights of two objects, and to determine which is heavier;

• recognizing the uses of such standard measuring tools as rulers, scales, and thermometers, and the language that matches the tools (pounds and ounces measure weight, inches and feet measure length);

• using measuring cups and spoons as part of a cooking project, and accurately reading the amounts.

Second Grade

2 Uses common instruments for measuring.

Second graders can be expected to know the purpose of certain common measurement instruments (such as balance scales, thermometers, and rulers). They are likely to be more successful solving problems using non-standard measures than standard measures because standard measures require the reading of calibrated scales. They should be developing a sense of measurement reference frames (such as about 1 lb., 1 ft.). Examples of children showing interest in and exploring the use of measurement instruments are:

• using a balance scale to determine which of two objects is heavier or lighter;

• recognizing the uses of such standard measuring tools as rulers, scales, and thermometers, and the language that matches the tools (pounds and ounces measure weight, inches and feet measure length);

• beginning to link measures to personal references (four hamburgers weigh about a pound, the notebook is about a foot high, water freezes at about 30 degrees).

Third Grade

2 Uses common instruments for accurate measuring.

Third graders can identify and use common instruments for measuring when solving measurement problems. They can be expected to read calibrated scales and begin to recognize that measurements often fall between whole numbers. Examples of how children use measuring devices effectively include:

• using a meter stick or a yardstick to measure the classroom perimeter;

• using a thermometer to measure indoor and outdoor temperature;

• estimating the weight of objects, then using a scale and reading both the number of pounds and ounces accurately.

Fourth Grade

2 Uses common instruments for accurate measuring.

Nine year olds are now familiar with common instruments used for measurement. They can be expected to use them flexibly and appropriately and to use fractional parts of whole numbers as they actually measure. Tools they can use include thermometers, scales, rulers, yardsticks, trundle wheels, and clocks. Examples include:

• keeping time using a stopwatch and recording information (for example, timing the 100 yard dash, putting a Tangram puzzle together, computing 100 simple multiplication math facts);

• making modeling clay using a balance with gram mass pieces to weigh ingredients;

• locating objects in the classroom that are a given length (5", 18", 26", and 52", etc.) then comparing results with classmates;

• conducting field observations of brooks, ponds, and streams and collecting data including temperature variations over time.

Fifth Grade

2 Uses common instruments for accurate measuring.

By the time students are ten years old, they should be familiar with a wide variety of tools commonly used for measuring. Their actual measurements should be precise because they can use and read small units (milliliters, grams, ounces). Examples include:

• using a stopwatch to record elapsed times of various events (running the 100-meter dash, tying a shoe five times, putting a Tangram puzzle together);

• estimating and then finding the mass of 10 different objects in standard units;

• using a protractor to measure and create angles;

• creating and using a sundial.

III Mathematical Thinking

E Measurement continued

Kindergarten

4 Shows a beginning understanding of time.

It is difficult for five year olds to understand the concept of time — to know the length of an hour or a week. They begin to refer to time in more conceptual terms by:

• referring to the trip taken when "I went to school the day before this one";

• commenting that planting the seeds took all of free-choice time;

• referring to going outside after lunch;

• knowing that it is winter because there is snow outside;

• telling a friend that "April is when my birthday comes and I will be six years old";

• discussing with a classmate the characteristics of a season, such as winter or summer;

• beginning to use appropriate words related to time and sequence in conversation.

First Grade

3 Shows beginning understanding of time and uses some time-related words.

First graders' beginning understanding of time includes reading and using information on a calendar with some accuracy. Examples of this understanding include:

• being able to name the days the class goes to gym;

• recognizing repeating patterns of time (days, weeks, and months);

• making reasonable estimates of amounts of time (it would take one second to throw a ball, one hour to bake a cake, one month to grow a bean plant);

• ordering their day ("I wake up at 6 a.m., I go to school at 7 a.m., I go to sleep at 8 p.m.").

Second Grade

3 Reads clocks and uses time-related words with relative accuracy.

Second graders can be expected to read and use calendar information purposefully. They can recognize familiar durations of time and tell time somewhat accurately to the hour and half hour. Examples of this include:

• reading the calendar and stating that Nov. 7, a Tuesday, is his brother's birthday;

• recognizing repeating patterns of time (days, weeks, months, years, and seasons);

• making reasonable estimates about amounts of time (it would take 10 minutes to run a mile, a half hour to ride the bus to school, or about one month to grow a bean plant);

• ordering their day ("I wake up at 6:30 a.m., I go to school at 7:30 a.m., I go to sleep at 8:30 p.m.");

• observing that it is almost 11:30, and that's when it is time for lunch.

Third Grade

3 Reads time on a clock and uses time-related words accurately.

Third graders can recognize and use methods to keep track of time (calendars, clocks). They can be expected to tell time somewhat accurately using both analog and digital clocks. Examples of their understanding of time include:

• recognizing repeating patterns of time (days, weeks, months, years, and seasons);

• making predictions of when events will occur, using calendars;

• estimating durations of time and checking estimates using a stop watch;

• ordering her/his day, week, or year ("In the fall I start school; after the winter holiday we will study mammals; there are three months until summer; my science project is due in two weeks.");

• telling time on digital and analog clocks.

Fourth Grade

No equivalent performance indicator at this level.

Fifth Grade

No equivalent performance indicator at this level.

III Mathematical Thinking

F Probability and statistics

Kindergarten

1 Collects data and makes records using lists or graphs.

Five year olds are just beginning to understand how pieces of abstract information can be arranged in coherent patterns. Teacher guidance is needed to help them begin to record their observations on lists or graphs. Examples include:

• making a line on the chart beside the bean plant to record its growth;

• setting up a chart in the block area to record who chooses to use blocks each day;

• listing the foods given to the hamster each day, then marking which foods were eaten and which were not;

• creating a chart with the teacher about the foods children bring for lunch;

• taking polls in the class and charting the results with teacher guidance.

First Grade

1 Collects and records data using simple tallies, lists, charts, and graphs.

First graders can conduct simple surveys and create real or concrete graphs. They can be expected to set up a real graph using one-to-one correspondence. Science and social studies experiences can provide opportunities for children to see the purposeful use of graphing as a way to organize information. Examples of this emerging skill include:

• designing a simple class survey and using it to collect data (for example, about favorite foods, number of brothers and sisters);

• tallying collected data (on questions such as, how many children want apples or bananas for snack?);

• creating a concrete or "real graph" (such as making a graph of "How we get to school" using green unifix cubes for bus and red ones for car, and yellow ones for walk) or a simple picture graph (pictures of buses, cars, and feet);

• setting up a graph in one-to-one correspondence with objects.

Second Grade

1 Collects and records data using tallies, lists, charts, and graphs.

Seven year olds can survey and collect data and then organize it into simple graphs. Science and social experiences provide opportunities for children to view graphing as a way to organize information. Examples of children's understanding of informational organization include:

• conducting a class survey and collecting data (for example, about favorite foods, number of brothers and sisters);

• tallying collected data (on questions such as how many children want to play kickball, tether ball, or jump rope at recess?);

• creating picture, bar, and line graphs;

• setting up a graph in one-to-one correspondence (for example, can line up data on a picture graph showing the types of shoes worn, and the number of each type);

• generating problems that involve collecting and organizing information.

Third Grade

1 Collects and records data using tallies, lists, charts, and graphs.

Many eight year olds have had experience collecting data (while keeping score in a game or tallying votes). They can invent some of their own ways to organize information, including making lists, charts, tallies, and graphs. Science and social experiences provide opportunities for children to view graphing as a way to organize information. Examples of children's understanding of informational organization include:

• conducting a class survey and collecting data (for example, about favorite sports, number of brothers and sisters);

• observing and graphing temperature changes over time;

• keeping track of time spent on homework each night and creating a bar graph from the data;

• participating in a discussion about how best to organize data collected from a survey;

• generating problems that involve collecting and organizing information.

Fourth Grade

1 Collects and organizes data using tallies, lists, charts, and graphs.

Most nine year olds have had some experience collecting and organizing data. They can design methods to record information, including the use of tally sheets to keep score in games, making graphs to record survey results, or charting data collected from interviews. They should be expected to know when to use different kinds of graphs. Examples include:

• reading, interpreting, and creating graphs using pictures, bars, lines, and forms;

• performing simple probability experiments;

• using tools (calculators, computers) to process and verify data;

• observing and describing data collected over a period of time (temperature and weather patterns during the school year);

• planning a class survey, graphing the data, and listing conclusions.

Fifth Grade

1 Uses tables, charts, and graphs to collect, record, and analyze data.

Fifth graders can choose from a variety of ways to organize and represent collected data, and explain their reasons for choosing specific formats. They can collect facts in an organized way and analyze the data. Ways that students demonstrate this skill include:

• designing and conducting a survey of students in the school to determine their opinions about a current event, graphing the collected data, and listing conclusions;

• observing and describing data collected during a period of time (for example, effects of air pollution on plant life);

• using graphs and charts in research projects (creating a graph that represents the increasing number of endangered species);

• creating, reading, and interpreting picture, line, bar, and pie graphs.

III Mathematical Thinking

III Mathematical Thinking

F Probability and statistics continued

Kindergarten	First Grade	Second Grade
No equivalent performance indicator at this level.	2 Reads a simple graph or chart and bases conclusions on it.	2 Reads graphs and charts, and bases conclusions and predictions on them.

Kindergarten

No equivalent performance indicator at this level.

First Grade

2 **Reads a simple graph or chart and bases conclusions on it.**

By reading and interpreting information from a graph, first graders begin to recognize that data can be organized and displayed in different ways. Some ways children demonstrate this skill include:

• saying how many children have birthdays in each month after reading a graph;

• developing a graph that describes types of houses and using it to answer questions (for example, "Which type of house do the most, the fewest, and equal numbers of students live in?");

• observing and describing how many days we have been in school.

Second Grade

2 **Reads graphs and charts, and bases conclusions and predictions on them.**

By second grade, children can read information from a graph and begin to make simple interpretations and predictions. Some ways children demonstrate this skill include:

• noticing patterns and relationships on a graph;

• answering questions using the information shown on the graph;

• observing and describing data collected over a period of time (such as, how high has bean plant A grown?);

• predicting coin tosses after reviewing charted information.

Third Grade

2 Reads graphs or charts, and bases conclusions and predictions on them.

When third graders have repeated opportunities to read and create graphs, they can interpret information from a graph and make predictions. Some ways children demonstrate this skill include:

• noticing patterns on a weather graph;

• predicting what might happen next after studying a graph that shows the results of successive coin tosses;

• observing and describing data collected over a period of time;

• comparing information organized into a series of different graph types (such as line, bar, pie).

Fourth Grade

2 Interprets different types of graphs and charts.

When nine year olds have repeated experiences in reading and creating graphs, they can analyze them and generate questions on their own. Children should be able to review a graph or chart and determine the topic and purpose. They can make predictions and draw conclusions from the information. Ways that students demonstrate these skills include:

• creating graphs using pictures, bars, lines, and pie graphs;

• collecting and organizing data in a systematic order, then interpreting data;

• performing and reporting on a variety of probability experiments (rolling doubles with two six-sided dice);

• observing and describing data collected over a period of time (effects of acid rain).

Fifth Grade

No equivalent performance indicator at this level.

III Mathematical Thinking

F Probability and statistics continued

Kindergarten

No equivalent performance indicator at this level.

First Grade

No equivalent performance indicator at this level.

Second Grade

No equivalent performance indicator at this level.

Third Grade

No equivalent performance indicator at this level.

Fourth Grade

No equivalent performance indicator at this level.

Fifth Grade

2 Shows an understanding of probability.

Fifth grade students can design experiments to determine probability and can discuss the relationship between probability and predictions. They gain an understanding of the connection between statistics and probability by working with data to show the frequency or likelihood of an event. Examples include:

• performing and reporting on a variety of probability experiments (with dice or coins);

• devising and carrying out a probability experiment;

• studying a sample of a collection and making predictions about the entire collection.

III Mathematical Thinking

Scientific Thinking

This domain addresses ways of thinking and inquiring about the natural and physical world. Emphasized are the processes of scientific investigation, because process skills are embedded in and fundamental to all science instruction and content. The domain's focus is on how children actively investigate through observing, recording, describing, questioning, forming explanations, and drawing conclusions.

IV Scientific Thinking

A Observing and investigating

Kindergarten

1 Uses senses to observe characteristics and behaviors of living and non-living things.

For five year olds, the first step in scientific thinking involves using their senses to observe their environment. At this age, the goal is to encourage curiosity and interest rather than seeking correct answers. Children become familiar with their physical world when they are able to observe, manipulate, and experiment. Children show their observational skills by:

• noticing that bubbles move up through the tube of water;

• noting the different ways that insects move (for example, by crawling, hopping, and flying);

• exploring the way that corn meal (in the sand table) feels on their hands, and describing its texture and how it flows;

• inspecting the bird's nest carefully and wondering about how it was constructed;

• smelling flowers and commenting on their different smells.

First Grade

1 Observes characteristics and behavior of living and non-living things.

Young children automatically use their senses to observe what is around them. Six year olds begin to recognize that closer observation provides more information. Some ways six year olds demonstrate developing observation skills include:

• responding to opportunities to explore and observe the physical attributes of plants and animals (habits of class pets, physical features of plants);

• spending time making observations and noting more than obvious details (such as counting the brown guinea pig's stripes and then looking for markings on the one that appears to be pure white);

• observing the properties of objects (for example, feeling the differences in the texture of clay before and after water is added);

• using all their observational senses (listening to outdoor sounds, smelling the odors of different liquids, feeling the textures of stones).

Second Grade

1 Observes characteristics and behavior of living and non-living things.

Young children automatically use their senses to observe what they see around them. Seven year olds can be expected to observe carefully, taking time to notice details, not just to focus on the obvious. Examples of their expanding observation skills are:

• devoting time and effort to observations, and noting more than the obvious features (for example, observing the particular colorations of rock samples, not simply size and shape);

• using all their observational senses appropriately (listening carefully to detect pitch differences created by differing amounts of liquid in a jar, or weighing rock samples as a way of comparing them);

• observing carefully to see how physical properties may affect action or behavior (seeing if the metal marble travels down the ramp faster or slower than the glass one).

Third Grade

1 **Observes characteristics and behavior of living and non-living things.**

Eight year olds can be expected to observe objects and events carefully, noting details, and not just to focus on the obvious. They should begin to recognize the benefits of taking time for observations and that it is often necessary to observe phenomena on multiple occasions in order to validate findings. Examples of their expanding observation skills include:

• carefully observing the hermit crab each day over the course of a week to see if it eats at particular times of day;

• making appropriate observational use of senses other than sight (touching food samples to compare their texture now with how they felt before they were left out for several days);

• observing several objects, looking for comparisons (watching plant growth under differing conditions).

Fourth Grade

1 **Observes characteristics and behaviors of living and non-living things.**

Nine year olds can be expected to observe carefully and with increasing accuracy. Their observation goes beyond noting obvious features of living and non-living things. By fourth grade, students observe similarities and differences and can articulate what they observe. Examples of observation skills include:

• devoting time and effort to observations and documenting discoveries and ideas;

• using tools for more detailed observations (for example, hand lenses, microscopes, standard measuring tools);

• documenting observations in a log;

• formulating ideas based on observations.

Fifth Grade

1 **Observes objectively, notices details, and orders observations.**

Ten year olds' increasingly deliberate observation skills allow them to note very specific and detailed information. Their ability to apply prior knowledge and observation techniques to new situations enables them to be more independent in their observations. They can connect current observations to objects and phenomena observed in the past. Examples of their expanding observation skills include:

• looking at a plant part under a microscope and observing and recording cell structure;

• observing and recording the color, height, and formation of clouds over a period of time and beginning to make weather-related predictions;

• examining a cow heart and comparing its structure to a diagram of a human heart, and recording information about similarities and differences.

IV Scientific Thinking

Ⅳ Scientific Thinking

A Observing and investigating continued

Kindergarten

2 Uses tools to gather information.

At five years old, children are very interested in using tools such as lenses or magnifying glasses, which they associate with grown-up activities. Scientific tools are not limited to observational tools but also include locomotion devices (gears, pulleys), technological tools, and measurement devices. Ways that children show their growing interest in scientific tools include:

• looking at all kinds of things through a hand lens;

• exploring weights with balance scales;

• experimenting with tubes and funnels at the sand and water tables;

• examining a bicycle chain and gear sprockets and trying to figure out how they make the wheels turn;

• looking through a bird guidebook to find the name of a bird seen outside the window.

First Grade

2 Recognizes some ways tools can be used to gather scientific information.

First graders can begin to use tools to help them gather scientific data. Whether it is a scale, container, or magnifier, they should think about how the tool is used as well as why it helps them with their scientific investigation. Examples of first graders gaining familiarity with scientific tools include:

• coming up with the proper tools and devices to help with an observation (placing an insect in a jar, covering the jar with aluminum foil, and using a pencil to poke holes in the foil so that the insect can breathe);

• using a magnifier to observe the structure of a bird's nest more closely;

• using a balance scale to compare the weights of rocks.

Second Grade

2 Recognizes some ways tools can be used to gather scientific information.

Second graders can be expected to use tools to help them gather scientific data. Whether it is a scale, thermometer, container, glass slide, or magnifier, they should be thinking about how the tool is used as well as why it helps them with their scientific investigation. Examples of how they use scientific tools include:

• wanting to find out how much weight a block structure can hold and realizing that the balance scale would be less effective than the calibrated scale;

• using a magnifier to observe the details of the caterpillar chrysalis;

• separating fabric fibers with tweezers to examine them more closely.

Third Grade

2 Recognizes some ways tools can be used to gather scientific information.

Third graders begin to understand that particular tools help us observe things that are too small or too far away to see, and that other tools are used for measuring. By this age, children should have opportunities to select tools that best serve their purposes as well as developing skills for using them. Examples of how they use scientific tools include:

• using thermometers to measure water temperature;

• deciding which size measuring cups to use to get exact amounts of liquids for a recipe;

• making a slide of a hair to examine under the microscope.

Fourth Grade

2 Recognizes ways tools can be used to gather scientific information.

Fourth graders are familiar with the use of some scientific tools. They are beginning to further their understanding of how tools allow scientists to explore phenomena. By this age children should be able to use tools to help them make scientific observations. Examples include:

• using hand lenses to observe insects;

• creating a microscope slide to examine soil bacteria;

• using pH papers to determine acid rain levels;

• using scales to measure weights of pendulum balls.

Fifth Grade

2 Uses tools with some accuracy to gather scientific information.

Fifth graders understand that tools allow them to measure and observe objects and phenomena that would otherwise be difficult to examine (microscopes to analyze cells, binoculars to identify birds, thermometers to determine water temperature variations). Examples include:

• using an audiometer to measure sound waves;

• using scalpel, tweezers, and pins to examine the internal anatomy of a snake;

• using litmus paper to test the pH of rainwater.

IV Scientific Thinking

IV Scientific Thinking

A Observing and investigating continued

Kindergarten	First Grade	Second Grade
3 Makes comparisons among objects that have been observed.	**3 Classifies and compares living and non-living things in different ways.**	**3 Classifies and compares living and non-living things in different ways.**

Kindergarten

After observing their environment, children need adult help to organize their observations into thoughts that will assist them in making further discoveries. They enjoy the challenge of sorting objects, seeing patterns in nature, noticing differences and similarities, drawing what they see, and dictating stories that describe their observations. Ways that children show they are making comparisons and organizing observations include:

• noting differences between wet and dry sand, and using wet and dry sand in different ways when building sand structures;

• looking for patterns in fall leaves and wondering why some leaves turn red and others turn yellow;

• categorizing animals into groups that move by hopping, by running, and by flying;

• becoming more accurate and precise when reporting observations;

• comparing different textures of materials put out for collage.

First Grade

Six year olds can be expected to sort and classify collections (rocks, magnets, leaves). This process helps them to observe more carefully. They can sort and classify by pre-existing and self-created categories. Evidence of this skill includes:

• noting similarities and differences among objects in a collection and naming groups based on attributes (things that are alive and not alive, plants and animals, things that swing, and things that bounce);

• putting objects into existing categories and providing a rationale for doing so;

• classifying according to opposite properties (sinking and floating, alive and not alive, heavy and light).

Second Grade

As children sort and classify what they are observing, they look at things more carefully. By seven, children can be expected to classify based on observation as well as on prior knowledge and experience. Examples of this skill include:

• noting similarities and differences among groups of things and naming groups based on the findings (low- and high-pitched sounds, water soluble and insoluble substances);

• classifying according to opposite properties (sinking and floating, alive and not alive, heavy and light);

• putting objects into existing categories and providing a rationale for doing so;

• measuring objects and classifying them by size or weight.

Third Grade

3 Classifies, categorizes, and compares living and non-living things in different ways.

As children observe, they can classify objects and phenomena into sets and subsets using pre-existing and self-created categories. By age eight, children are likely to classify based on observation as well as on prior knowledge and experience. Examples of this skill include:

• classifying by specific properties (animals with and without backbones, plants with and without stems, machines using levers or pulleys or inclined planes);

• putting objects into existing categories and providing their rationale for doing so;

• graphing observations over time and then using the information from the graph to classify further observations.

Fourth Grade

3 Classifies, categorizes, and compares living and non-living things in different ways.

Nine year old students continue to classify objects and phenomena into sets and subsets. Their classifications are based on what they observe, and show the application of previously learned concepts and knowledge to new situations. By this age, students should recognize that an important purpose of classification is the identification of likenesses and differences. Noticing similarities and differences and trying to explain them is a critical part of the scientific process. A student demonstrates these skills by:

• classifying according to specific properties (identifying characteristics of various leaves: palmate, pinnate, parallel);

• putting objects into already existing categories and explaining their rationale for doing this (identifying types of rocks and minerals: granite, sandstone, shale, limestone, gneiss, quartz, feldspar, mica);

• graphing observations over a period of time and then using the information from the graph to make comparisons.

Fifth Grade

3 Classifies, categorizes and compares living and non-living things in different ways.

Ten year olds are increasingly able to think abstractly and as a result can deal with hypothetical situations. They are learning to use multiple classifications and to understand that problems can be solved in ordered and quantitative ways. Examples include:

• classifying according to specific properties (cells that produce their own food and those that do not);

• putting objects into pre-existing categories and explaining the rationale for doing this (grouping shells by shape: conical, rectangular, circular, elongated, irregular);

• classifying rocks using a variety of testing techniques (scratching to determine hardness, testing for acidity, observing color).

IV Scientific Thinking

Kindergarten

4 Seeks answers to questions through active investigation.

Children this age need help knowing where to find answers or how to understand their observations. Some ways children seek information include:

• trying to understand why water flows up when it is siphoned out of the water table;

• tracking observations on charts or by drawing what they see;

• figuring out ways (with the teacher's help) that they can investigate phenomena they have observed;

• designing experiments to discover information about such things as floating and sinking, magnets, and batteries and bulbs;

• recalling observations and looking through books to chart the various ways people move around (using escalators, elevators, trains, planes, buses).

First Grade

4 Seeks information by active investigation.

The process of investigation includes collecting, counting, and measuring things, and organizing information in ways that make interpretation easier. Children often pose questions that they can begin to answer through careful observation, by setting up simple "tests" and by applying previously learned scientific knowledge to new situations. However, they may still need teacher encouragement and support to do so. Examples include:

• setting out different food samples and observing which foods the hamster prefers;

• collecting many different types of pine cones so as to have a large sample to sort and classify;

• looking at pictures and captions in books and magazines to find information related to a particular question;

• using a balance scale to weigh various items to test a theory that the bigger something is, the more it weighs.

Second Grade

4 Seeks information by active investigation.

The process of investigation includes collecting, counting, and measuring things, and organizing information in ways that make interpretation easier. Second graders who have experienced some scientific investigation can begin to answer questions through various techniques, including setting up simple "tests" and applying previously learned scientific knowledge to new situations. Examples include:

• using focused observation to answer specific questions (watching the frog to see how it catches and eats crickets);

• using books, magazines, and charts to help answer questions;

• setting up experiments to test theories (leaving bowls with the same amount of water in different parts of the classroom and monitoring how long it takes for the water in each bowl to evaporate);

• making a chart of how much water evaporated each day to help organize observations.

Third Grade

4 Seeks information by active investigation.

The process of investigation includes collecting, counting, and measuring things, and organizing information in ways that make interpretation easier. Third graders who have experienced some scientific investigation can be expected to answer questions by various techniques, including setting up simple "tests" and applying previously learned scientific knowledge to new situations. Examples include:

• setting up a test to see which magnet is strongest;

• using books, magazines, and charts to find information that supports a hypothesis;

• designing an investigation, including control of one or two variables (testing to see how fast the ball rolls when the angle of the ramp or size of the ball changes);

• integrating new information with existing knowledge (finding out something new about how the filter in the fish tank works and relating it to previous information);

• using computer databases to explore a topic.

Fourth Grade

4 Seeks answers to questions by active investigation.

Nine year olds begin to develop an understanding of the type of investigation (observation, collection, experimentation) required to answer certain types of questions. They continue to collect, measure, and organize their information and can conduct tests that include up to two variables as they rely upon previously acquired knowledge. Examples of active investigation are:

• designing an investigation, including control of two or three variables and predicting how the variables will affect outcomes (determining which factors affect plant growth, what effect various acids have on teeth, or which towel is most absorbent);

• using reference materials to pursue questions;

• drawing on experiences and knowledge to make more accurate predictions;

• making and testing hypotheses with experimentation (predicting which medium mold is likely to grow best on: leather, plastic, wood, butter).

Fifth Grade

4 Shows some understanding of how to use the scientific method.

Fifth graders should be able to apply the scientific method independently. After they pose a question they can state what they already know, make a prediction, create a plan to investigate, complete the investigation, and record and communicate their findings to others. They can be expected to ask questions such as "what works?" "what didn't work?" "where do I go from here?" and "what do I know now that I didn't know before?" Examples include:

• predicting the basic survival needs of plants and creating experiments using different quantities of water and light;

• creating a bridge out of toothpicks and testing its design for strength and balance;

• measuring acidity levels in common substances (lemon juice, vinegar, milk, club soda, rainwater);

• observing the structure of a collection of seeds and drawing some conclusions about the factors involved in their dispersal.

IV Scientific Thinking

IV Scientific Thinking

B Questioning and predicting

Kindergarten

1 Expresses wonder and seeks information about the natural world.

Most five-year olds do not need much coaching or prodding to learn to ask "why?" But they need help to focus their observations and to use observational processes that will generate new information. They show their growing interest in scientific investigation by:

• working with wheeled vehicles, slopes, and differently-shaped objects to find out how inanimate objects move;

• exploring where animals live by studying such homes as caves, nests, and burrows;

• bringing in a collection of stones found on the way to school and looking at them through a magnifying glass, noting differences and investigating what gives some of them white streaks and some of them sparkles;

• bringing in insects, bird nests, or seeds to show the class and to investigate.

First Grade

1 Asks questions about the natural and physical world.

Children demonstrate their natural curiosity by the types of questions they ask and the ways they engage in scientific investigation. Modeling helps first graders ask scientific questions that extend "why" to "what" and "how" ("How could we find out?", "What would happen if…?"), leading to possible investigation. Evidence of their developing sense of scientific questions includes:

• bringing some seeds to school and posing questions that can be answered by observation and experimentation;

• completing a study of small creatures in which they observe which body parts insects use to get their food, and then asking if plants have certain parts that help them get food;

• experimenting with yeast, and then trying to find out why certain kinds of bread get soft and puffy while others get hard and crusty.

Second Grade

1 Asks questions about the natural and physical world.

Children demonstrate their natural curiosity by the types of questions they ask and the ways they engage in scientific investigation. Second graders are still likely to need modeling to help them ask scientific questions — ones that extend "why" to "what" and "how" questions ("How could we find out?", "What would happen if…?"), leading to possible investigation. Evidence of their developing sense of scientific questions includes:

• asking questions that go beyond the superficial and obvious features of an event or experience;

• posing "what" and "how" questions about what is not directly observable ("What are the effects of water pollution?", "What has caused certain species of animals to become endangered?");

• completing an investigation, and then posing new and more in-depth questions (after observing snails, asking if their shells serve other purposes besides protection).

Third Grade

1 **Asks questions about the natural and physical world.**

Children demonstrate their natural curiosity by the types of questions they ask and the ways they engage in scientific investigation. Third graders with prior science experience can be expected to recognize scientific questions — ones that can lead to a scientific investigation (for example, questions that extend "why" to "what" and "how"). Third graders demonstrate an understanding of scientific questions by:

• asking a series of related questions that extend beyond the superficial and obvious features of an event or experience;

• responding thoughtfully to a teacher's question, such as, "How could you find out what frogs eat?";

• after sorting and classifying materials, asking a "what would happen if" question and then thinking through how to set up an experiment to find out.

Fourth Grade

1 **Formulates scientific questions about the physical and natural world.**

Most nine year olds have explored the physical and natural world within their classroom or neighborhood. By fourth grade they can begin to distinguish between "how" and "why" questions in their formal and informal investigations through discussions, research, and further experimentation. Some examples of a student's ability to formulate questions about the physical and natural world include:

• recognizing the differences between questions that can or cannot be investigated (whether it is possible to find out how much oxygen is produced by a plant during photosynthesis);

• asking detailed questions that arise from a particular study (plants, invertebrates);

• using systematic questioning to analyze why two groups of children obtained differing results in an experiment.

Fifth Grade

1 **Formulates scientific questions about the physical and natural world.**

By asking questions and attempting to answer them through active investigations, ten year olds can be more creative in their thinking processes and attempt to solve problems objectively and systematically. Examples include:

• designing scientific models that reflect a personal interest;

• seeking information about what is not directly observable (for example, designing and carrying out an experiment related to the study of a musical instrument's sound waves);

• researching questions that have inconclusive answers ("Is the Earth entering a state of global warming?").

IV Scientific Thinking

Ⅳ Scientific Thinking

B Questioning and predicting continued

Kindergarten	First Grade	Second Grade
No equivalent performance indicator at this level.	**2 Makes logical predictions when pursuing scientific investigations.**	**2 Makes logical predictions when pursuing scientific investigations.**

Kindergarten

No equivalent performance indicator at this level.

First Grade

2 Makes logical predictions when pursuing scientific investigations.

Children often make predictions at the outset of an investigation ("What do you think will happen if I make the airplane wings longer?") and then again after they have gathered some data. Using logic, paying close attention to details, and recalling prior knowledge all contribute to the kinds of predictions children make. First graders can make thoughtful predictions and not simply wild guesses. Examples of their beginning skills are:

• drawing on prior experiences to make predictions (for example, "The caterpillar took about a week to come out of its chrysalis, but I think the chicks will take longer to hatch because they are bigger.");

• observing patterns and using them to help make predictions;

• making logical but erroneous predictions as a result of careful observation ("I don't think the Styrofoam will float because it is solid and all the other things we tested so far that were solid sank.").

Second Grade

2 Makes logical predictions when pursuing scientific investigations.

Children often make predictions at the outset of an investigation ("What do you think will happen if...") and then again after they have gathered some data. Using logic, paying close attention to details, and recalling prior knowledge all contribute to the kinds of predictions children make. Second graders can begin to reflect on their predictions and not simply make wild guesses. Examples of their prediction skills might include:

• drawing on prior knowledge to make predictions (for example, having experimented with wires and batteries before, predicting that the bulb will light up only if the wires are hooked up in a particular way);

• after sorting and classifying a group of objects, studying them before predicting which are magnetic and which are not;

• making a prediction and then revising it after additional observation and experience.

Third Grade

2 Makes logical predictions when pursuing scientific investigations.

The more experience children have with scientific investigation, the more likely they are to make logical predictions. Third graders with some scientific experience are likely to look for patterns to help guide their predictions. Examples of how they demonstrate their prediction skills are:

• trying out a series of different levers and carefully observing what they do before making a prediction about how a completely different one would work;

• recalling experience and prior knowledge to predict the movement of a river;

• studying a graph depicting growth and then making a prediction about what will happen next.

Fourth Grade

2 Makes logical predictions when pursuing scientific investigations.

Children of this age are increasingly able to integrate their prior scientific knowledge about the world with their ongoing investigations. Nine year olds continue to look for more complex patterns and begin to make predictions and hypotheses based on their observations. Examples of a student's ability to predict and hypothesize include:

• making and testing predictions with experimentation (designing clay boats and determining whether they will float and how much weight they can carry);

• discussing predictions and hypotheses with others;

• drawing on experiences and knowledge to make more accurate predictions.

Fifth Grade

2 Uses evidence and prior knowledge to make logical scientific predictions.

Ten year olds can be expected to become more skilled at gathering pertinent information and developing increasingly detailed explanations using abstract reasoning. These skills allow them to make inferences and interpret information that leads to logical predictions. Examples include:

• drawing on experiences and knowledge to arrive at more accurate predictions;

• making and testing predictions about future phenomena (predicting weather from cloud formations).

IV Scientific Thinking

IV Scientific Thinking

C Explaining and forming conclusions

Kindergarten	First Grade	Second Grade

Kindergarten

1 Forms explanations based on observations and explorations.

Scientific thinking requires observation, drawing conclusions, and proposing explanations about future events. Children can begin to guess the reasons for what they have observed — even if those reasons are not "scientifically correct" — as they organize, with teacher support and guidance, the information they have gathered. Evidence of this thinking includes:

• explaining that a conch shell has all those bumps and prongs so that there will be more room inside;

• guessing that a sponge will sink in the water because it is bigger than a plastic boat that floated;

• offering an explanation for why colors mixed together create new colors;

• guessing what conditions (such as water, light, and fertilizer) will help a plant grow;

• predicting that a classroom pet will or will not eat certain foods;

• designing an investigation and repeating it several times to test predictions.

First Grade

1 Forms explanations and conclusions based on observation and experimentation.

Critical to the process of scientific investigation is the ability to use observations and information to construct reasonable explanations. Six year olds are likely to need encouragement and modeling to learn how to respond to the question, "Why do you think this happened?" Some ways children show evidence of this emerging skill are:

• deciding which type of material bounces highest by dropping different kinds of balls from various heights and recording the findings;

• describing the best growing conditions for a plant, after systematically varying light, water, and growing medium;

• developing ideas about circuits by experimenting with batteries and bulbs.

Second Grade

1 Forms explanations and conclusions based on observation and experimentation.

Critical to the process of scientific investigation is the ability to use observations and information to construct reasonable explanations. Seven year olds will need encouragement and modeling to learn how to respond to the question, "Why did this happen?" Some ways children show evidence of this skill are:

• after conducting several tests, explaining that wheels and inclined planes make work easier;

• describing the best growing conditions for a plant, after systematically varying light, water, and growing medium;

• developing ideas about types of materials that will disintegrate quickly after burying different objects in soil for several weeks.

Third Grade

1 Forms explanations and conclusions based on observation and experimentation.

Critical to the process of scientific investigation is the ability to use observations and information to construct reasonable explanations. Depending on prior experience, eight year olds may need encouragement and modeling to learn how to respond to the question, "Why did this happen?" Some ways a child shows evidence of this skill are:

• providing explanations about why certain objects need to be pushed and others pulled in order to get them to move;

• explaining how the earthworm moves, after carefully observing one for several days;

• recognizing a pattern on a graph showing when the moon was over their house each night and offering an explanation for it.

Fourth Grade

1 Draws conclusions based on observations and experimentation.

An integral aspect of the scientific process is drawing logical conclusions based on investigation, research, and prior knowledge. Nine year olds can start to give reasonable explanations about their observations and investigations independently and spontaneously. Some ways that students demonstrate these skills are:

• determining what mammals eat by studying their teeth or learning what birds eat by examining their beaks;

• hesitating to draw a conclusion without adequate information;

• developing ideas about what makes good or inadequate experimental designs;

• presenting revised explanations based on new information.

Fifth Grade

1 Draws conclusions based on observation and experimentation.

Ten year olds should be able to initiate probing questions such as "what caused this?", "what would happen if…?", or "how can you prove this?" to explain their findings. Children are expected to use several sources to create a hypothesis and to explain the thinking behind their reasoning. They can extend their thinking beyond a conclusion and initiate further questions. Ways children draw conclusions include:

• hesitating to draw a conclusion without adequate data;

• using factual information to explain an investigation or natural phenomena;

• developing some ideas about what makes a good or inadequate experimental design;

• using discussions with others to help formulate conclusions;

• creating charts and presenting evidence based on information discovered in investigations (for example, mercury is heavier than oxygen).

IV Scientific Thinking

IV Scientific Thinking

C Explaining and forming conclusions continued

Kindergarten	First Grade	Second Grade
No equivalent performance indicator at this level.	**2 Communicates scientific information in various ways.**	**2 Communicates scientific information in various ways.**

First Grade

2 Communicates scientific information in various ways.

As first graders observe, and as they conduct simple investigations, they can be expected to record what they are doing and seeing with drawings and simple captions. Children need opportunities to describe their findings and analyze them in discussions (for example, "Why did you decide to do it that way?" and "How do you know that's the reason?"). Examples of their increasing skills as communicators of scientific thinking include:

• using details in drawings to show specific characteristics (for example, plants of different sizes, colors, and leaf shapes);

• drawing and writing about the hermit crab and then explaining why they decided the hermit crab was angry;

• using words that convey differences in size, shape, and feel (the plant's leaves feel wet, cool, fuzzy, or smooth).

Second Grade

2 Communicates scientific information in various ways.

As children observe, and as they conduct experiments, they can be expected to record what they are doing and seeing in journals, logs, or on simple observation forms. Drawings, written descriptions, charts, and graphs can be created by second graders. Children need opportunities to describe their findings and analyze them in discussions (for example, "Why did you decide to do it that way?" and "How do you know that's the reason?"). Examples of their increasing skills as communicators of scientific thinking include:

• making drawings that are increasingly detailed and realistic;

• making a graph to record and describe information gathered over time and then explaining how they decided what kind of graph would best illustrate their findings;

• using words to convey mathematical concepts, such as size, weight, speed, and motion ("The large red ball floated, but the small stone sank quickly.").

Third Grade

2 Communicates scientific information in various ways.

As third graders observe, and as they conduct experiments, they can be expected to record what they are doing and seeing in journals, logs, or on simple observation forms. Appropriate drawings, written descriptions, charts, and graphs can be expected of third graders. Children need opportunities to describe their findings and analyze them in discussions (for example, "Why did you decide to do it that way?" and "How do you know that's the reason?"). Examples of their skills as recorders of scientific exploration include:

• making drawings that are increasingly detailed and realistic;

• making a graph to record and describe information gathered over time and then explaining how they decided what kind of graph would best illustrate their findings;

• using words to convey mathematical concepts, such as size, weight, speed, and motion ("The larger red ball floated, but the small stone sank fast.").

Fourth Grade

2 Describes, records, and explains findings.

By fourth grade, students are ready to use a variety of methods (drawings, logs, graphs, tables, and charts) to explain their findings. The most appropriate means of recording is not always obvious to nine year olds, and they will often need teacher assistance to help them think about the best way to record their information. Examples of a student's ability to record and describe findings include:

• writing ideas and responses to various questions or investigations in a journal;

• choosing an appropriate method for presenting results;

• using scientific vocabulary to explain ideas that were learned previously (indigenous, decomposer, potential energy);

• creating a graph to illustrate different kinds of rocks found on a field trip .

Fifth Grade

2 Describes, records, and explains findings.

Ten year olds use communication as a means to sort out ideas, link different experiences, describe events, and share ideas and information using drawings, journals, logs, graphs, tables, charts, and symbols to explain their thinking. Examples of these abilities include:

• using details in drawings that attempt to show relative size, shape, texture, shading, position, and complexity;

• using written and verbal descriptions of observations and ideas that are clear, complete, and accurate;

• graphing vital statistics (weight, size, color, and diet to make comparisons within a species);

• presenting findings to an audience using drawings, graphs, or other visual aids.

IV Scientific Thinking

C Explaining and forming conclusions continued

Kindergarten	First Grade	Second Grade
No equivalent performance indicator at this level.	No equivalent performance indicator at this level.	No equivalent performance indicator at this level.

Third Grade

No equivalent performance indicator at this level.

Fourth Grade

3 **Forms explanations that acknowledge interactive relationships between systems.**

Nine year olds are able to recognize the relationships between objects or events within a system (the human body, the solar system). Abstract concepts, such as interaction, become an important aspect of their inquiries. Examples include:

• showing the connections between two or more elements through various media (drawing a food chain, building a model showing planetary motion, creating a demonstration of soil erosion);

• explaining the relationship between an animal's coloration, environment, and predators;

• using a line graph to figure out the relationship between distance and time.

Fifth Grade

3 **Forms explanations that acknowledge interactive relationships between systems.**

Fifth graders can now extend their thinking to include systems and the interconnectedness of elements within a system. Their questions and conversations should show an understanding of how parts of a system interrelate to fulfill the system's function. Examples of this thinking include:

• writing a research report on a particular ecosystem;

• drawing pictures or building models that accurately illustrate systems and their components (ecosystem, solar system, body system);

• explaining the relationship among body systems with charts or diagrams.

IV Scientific Thinking

Social Studies

This domain emphasizes the acquisition of social and cultural understanding. Children acquire this understanding from personal experiences and by learning about the experiences of others. As children study present day and historical topics, they gain understanding of human interdependence and the relationships between people and their environment.

V Social Studies

A Human similarities and differences

Kindergarten

1 Begins to recognize self and others as having shared and different characteristics.

Five year old children may still be egocentric. They may not have had much opportunity to experience a range of different ethnic groups and lifestyles. Children may find differences frightening or uncomfortable. But their experience can be easily broadened by exploring the different characteristics of their classmates. Some ways this happens are:

• talking with a child with a hearing impairment to learn what can be heard with or without a hearing aid;

• exploring physical commonalities and differences (such as, everyone has hair, but hair comes in different colors, textures, and lengths);

• exploring heights of children in the class, making a chart and talking about the advantages of being tall or short;

• finding out why one child has trouble running and then explaining to another classmate the problem of walking and running when one leg is shorter than the other;

• exploring the use of canes, walkers, or wheelchairs.

First Grade

1 Recognizes self and others as having shared and different characteristics.

Six year olds may have had little experience with people who are different from themselves. Activities that foster thinking about themselves and their families (such as reading, discussions, and interviews) help them to recognize the qualities that make individuals both unique and similar (for example, physical characteristics, personal interests, and feelings); to develop respect for diversity (in cultural, gender, age, and other categories); and, to learn that people come from many different backgrounds. Evidence of their understanding of similarities and differences includes:

• expressing ideas related to relevant stories that were read aloud;

• making drawings, paintings, and puppets that reflect an awareness of physical differences;

• interacting easily with children who differ in obvious ways;

• observing similarities and differences in self-portraits, photographs, and illustrations.

Second Grade

1 Recognizes self and others as having shared and different characteristics.

Seven year olds may have had little experience with people who are different from themselves. They learn to recognize unique and shared qualities of individuals (such as physical characteristics, personal interests, and feelings) by studying themselves, their families, and literature. In this way, they develop respect for diversity (in culture, gender, age, and other categories) and learn that people come from many different backgrounds. Evidence of their understanding of similarities and differences includes:

• expressing ideas and opinions during classroom discussions;

• dramatizing stories and creating puppet plays in ways that reflect an awareness of individual similarities and differences;

• collaborating on a mural focusing on their schoolmates and incorporating a wide range of physical differences when depicting the children;

• expressing interest in a story character who is very different from themselves.

Third Grade

1 Recognizes self and others as having shared and different characteristics.

Eight year olds can explore human similarities and differences (such as physical characteristics, behaviors, motives, beliefs, hopes, and fears) in the present and the past. Through literature and other studies, they can contrast their own lives with others and learn that people come from many different backgrounds. Some ways they demonstrate understanding of the scope of personal diversity include:

• creating artwork that reflects an awareness of diversity (painting a picture that includes people whose race or culture differs from their own, or who are in wheelchairs);

• writing about a story character and reflecting on ways the character is both alike and different from themselves;

• noticing and commenting on an instance of bias in a story;

• dramatizing stories and creating puppet plays in ways that reflect awareness of individual similarities and differences.

Fourth Grade

1 Shows understanding of similarities and differences in how people conduct their lives.

Students in the fourth grade are learning about the world beyond their own communities. Human similarities can now be understood to include cultural similarities and differences. As children learn to make comparisons between themselves and others they can learn to appreciate the diversity of human experiences and how culture shapes people's lives. Examples of how nine year olds express an understanding and appreciation for cultural influences include:

• analyzing literature (novels, folktales, and myths) from or about various cultures and describing similarities and differences in beliefs (comparing mummification in ancient Egypt to current burial rituals);

• creating a family timeline that shows the origin of their ancestors and factors that influenced the migration of their people;

• interviewing another classmate about his/her family traditions and background;

• interviewing other classmates about their family traditions and backgrounds.

Fifth Grade

1 Shows understanding of similarities and differences in how people conduct their lives.

As fifth graders learn about the world beyond their own families and communities, they use their understanding of themselves and their heritage as a point of reference. Making comparisons between themselves and others encourages reflection about how culture shapes people's lives. Fifth graders consider how migration and immigration cause people of different cultures to influence one another. Examples of how fifth graders express this understanding include:

• analyzing literature (for example, novels, folktales, and myths) from or about various cultures and describing the similarities and differences of cultures and beliefs;

• writing stories in which the characteristics of central characters reflect understanding of another culture;

• creating artwork that realistically depicts scenes from an ancient culture.

V Social Studies

Kindergarten

2 Identifies similarities and differences in habits, patterns of living, and culture.

Five year olds are becoming more aware of their classmates' various cultures by observing their conversations, dramatic play interactions, and the things they bring to school from home. Children this age can begin to explore differences in lifestyles, and with experience, knowledge, and teacher support, can overcome their fear of differences and become excited and accepting about new ways of living. They show their growing interest and acceptance by:

• exploring the language bilingual children speak at home, and learning some of the words;

• tasting a snack that a classmate from another culture brings to school, and exploring its relationship to holidays and other special occasions;

• discussing with classmates the people with whom they live (sisters, aunts, grandparents, two mothers or fathers, only one parent);

• exploring through dramatic play the varied habits, celebrations, and lifestyles that classmates experience in their homes.

First Grade

2 Identifies similarities and differences in group habits and living patterns.

The way people live and behave is often influenced by the groups to which they belong. People are part of many different groups (family, classroom, culture, religion, community). First graders can begin to consider ways that membership in groups shapes people's lives (family structure, language, foods, dress, conflict resolution methods, celebrations). Examples of their growing understanding of similarities and differences in group behaviors include:

• building apartment houses like ones in the neighborhood with blocks and dramatizing scenes that reflect daily life in them;

• retelling a personal story about a family holiday celebration;

• listening to a story and then commenting that their family had to learn English just like the family in the story;

• visiting a friend from a single-parent home and then experimenting with ideas on different family structures by drawing pictures in a journal.

Second Grade

2 Identifies similarities and differences in group habits and living patterns.

The way people live and behave is often influenced by the groups to which they belong. People are part of many different groups (family, classroom, culture, religion, community). By looking at their own families and others in the community, second graders can explore how membership in groups shapes people's lives (family structure, language, foods, dress, conflict resolution methods, celebrations). Examples of how children reveal this understanding include:

• asking questions or offering opinions in a discussion about a story in which the character's lifestyle is different than one's own;

• making a model that reflects family life on a farm based on reading some historical fiction;

• sharing objects from home that describe family habits (photo albums, family artifacts);

• drawing and writing about life in their grandparents' country of origin.

Third Grade

2 Identifies similarities and differences in habits and living patterns now and in the past.

The way people live and behave is often influenced by the groups to which they belong. People are part of many different groups (family, classroom, culture, religion, community). Third graders who have thought about how their lives have been shaped by belonging to different groups (family structure, language, foods, dress, conflict resolution methods, celebrations), can make comparisons to people in other places or to those who lived long ago. Examples of how children reveal this understanding include:

• painting a mural representing lifestyles of long ago;

• writing a report based on an interview with a grandparent about life when he/she was a child;

• dramatizing the life experiences and feelings of people moving to a new homeland.

Fourth Grade

2 Shows some understanding of how human differences can result in conflict.

By fourth grade, many students have predetermined ideas about people that are based on culture, gender, or socio-economic stereotypes. They can be expected to understand that different experiences, beliefs, and values can lead to conflicts among friends, within and between families, communities, and nations. As nine year olds develop their interest in current or historical social issues and learn how to listen to different viewpoints they can begin to understand that very few complex social problems have simple answers. Some ways a student may demonstrate this understanding include:

• writing reports about the Civil Rights movement;

• mediating playground conflicts;

• dramatizing scenes based on the lives of human rights activists (Martin Luther King, Mahatma Gandhi);

• comparing the causes of a past war to the causes of a current conflict.

Fifth Grade

2 Shows understanding of how human differences can result in conflict.

Fifth grade students continue to learn that people's beliefs shape their political and social systems, now and in the past. They recognize some ways in which people negotiate differences, both peacefully and violently. As they examine events, past and present, they can reflect on two sides of a story and speculate about how and why conflict arises. Examples of this understanding include:

• analyzing a film or a piece of literature and discussing the role of prejudice and discrimination in the story;

• participating in a role play that depicts two opposing viewpoints about a historical conflict (between feudal lords and serfs, between Native Americans and colonists);

• writing a story based on research about historical conflict (religious intolerance in seventeenth-century England, apartheid in South Africa).

V Social Studies

149

V Social Studies

B Human interdependence

Kindergarten

1 Begins to understand family structures and roles.

Five year olds continue to explore various family roles and to examine other families to see how they differ from or are the same as their own. They continue to learn through dramatic play and in conversations with each other. Examples include:

• exploring family structures (for example, families differ in number and type of members);

• looking at classmates' family photos, and discussing the variety of family structures and membership;

• talking with a classmate about how each celebrates a coming holiday, such as Halloween, Memorial Day, or a special ethnic celebration;

• discussing, at the play dough table, the types of food eaten and enjoyed in each other's homes.

First Grade

No equivalent performance indicator at this level.

Second Grade

No equivalent performance indicator at this level.

Third Grade

No equivalent performance indicator at this level.

Fourth Grade

No equivalent performance indicator at this level.

Fifth Grade

No equivalent performance indicator at this level.

V Social Studies

B Human interdependence continued

Kindergarten

No equivalent performance indicator at this level.

First Grade

1 **Recognizes some ways people rely on each other for goods and services.**

As first graders explore different roles in the family, school, and community, they can be expected to see how people rely on others to get the goods and services they need. For example, all people need food, but some people produce it, some transport it, some sell it, and others just buy it. Examples of how first graders express this understanding includes:

• noticing that the character in a story earns his living by working in a courthouse the same way their mother does;

• sharing notes from interviews with family members about who does which chores in the family;

• following a trip to the zoo, drawing and writing about the different jobs people had;

• making a mural of the people who work in the supermarket.

Second Grade

1 **Recognizes some ways people rely on each other for goods and services.**

Examining different roles in their family, school, and the community enables second graders to recognize ways that people who live and function in groups depend on each other for goods and services. They can also be expected to show some understanding of how basic economic concepts relate to their lives. Examples of how second graders express this understanding include:

• relating personal experiences in the family or kin system to a piece of literature (for example, contrasting roles in one's own family with those of characters in a story);

• writing stories and research reports based on interviews with community workers;

• drawing or painting scenes depicting some ways people's roles in their jobs overlap (for example, at a factory, at the newspaper office, in the school);

• creating a web of all the jobs involved in getting milk to the supermarket.

Third Grade

1 Recognizes ways people rely on each other for goods and services now and in the past.

Drawing on their understanding and experiences of their own families and community, eight year olds begin to recognize the ways people in other places rely on one another for goods and services and the ways people in the past relied on one another for goods and services. They can be expected to show some understanding of how basic economic concepts affect people's lives. Examples of how they reveal these understandings include:

• creating a model representing how people traded goods and services in the local community 100 years ago;

• dramatizing scenes from historical fiction that depict family roles of long ago;

• participating in setting up a class newspaper and helping to create a scheme for labor division;

• writing a research report about how the food we eat gets to our tables.

Fourth Grade

1 Shows some understanding of how people rely on each other for economic needs.

Nine year olds can begin to extend their thinking and knowledge about the economics of their communities and reflect upon how people depend on each other for goods and services globally. Fourth graders can be expected to understand that all people rely on products produced in different areas of the world. Examples of this emergent thinking include:

• drawing a diagram of the steps that food goes through between farm and table;

• participating in a classroom simulation of a mini-community economy that includes stores, businesses, banks, and other services;

• interviewing a senior citizen to determine how people's needs and expectations have changed over time;

• writing a research report on how historical events have influenced economic events (the Great Depression, World War I);

• researching local businesses that have connections with other countries in the world.

Fifth Grade

1 Shows understanding of how all people rely on each other for economic needs.

As ten year olds study other cultures, past and present, they gain understanding of how all people meet basic needs by devising ways to live and work together. They begin to see how people turn to others when resources are scarce. Fifth graders demonstrate this understanding by:

• writing research reports about where and how food travels around the world to our supermarkets;

• conducting research about local industries to learn about production and distribution;

• simulating methods of trade used in the past (for example, apprenticeship and barter in the Middle Ages).

V Social Studies

V Social Studies

B Human interdependence continued

Kindergarten	First Grade	Second Grade
2 Describes some people's jobs and what is required to perform them.	**2 Begins to understand what people need to accomplish their jobs.**	**2 Shows understanding of what people need to accomplish their jobs.**

Kindergarten

2 Describes some people's jobs and what is required to perform them.

Five year olds are ready to examine their community and explore the many roles people fill in helping each other live. They are often excited to explore the mail delivery system or the garbage collection and disposal system. They are still interested in doctors, firefighters, and police officers. They show this interest by:

• pretending to be a store salesperson or mail carrier, involving others in this play, and asking questions about the way these jobs are performed and the tools they use;

• pretending to be the teacher, discussing why teachers are necessary, and exploring the many roles of a teacher;

• pretending to be their own father or mother, who goes to work outside the home, and figuring out what they do on their jobs;

• expressing in any art form (dramatic play, music, painting, blocks, sand) the role of a community worker, including descriptions of the tools needed to do the job.

First Grade

2 Begins to understand what people need to accomplish their jobs.

As first graders explore community businesses and services (local stores, the fire station, or a farm), they can begin to recognize what is involved in accomplishing work. Each job serves specific functions, requires specialized training, and may make use of tools, equipment, and machinery. Some ways children demonstrate this understanding include:

• creating a block building of the fire station and dramatizing how firefighters accomplish their tasks;

• drawing and writing a story about the baker's equipment based on a trip to the local bakery;

• building an assembly line made of Legos after a trip to an automobile factory;

• making detailed observations about the trucks and machines pictured in a book about the construction industry.

Second Grade

2 Shows understanding of what people need to accomplish their jobs.

As they explore community businesses and services (the sanitation department, power station, railroad), second graders can think about what is involved in accomplishing work. Each job serves specific functions, requires specialized training, and may make use of tools, equipment, and machinery. Second graders demonstrate this understanding by:

• writing up an interview with the school's custodian about his/her job duties;

• making a chart or graph showing all the machines found during a trip to a large office building;

• telling the class about a conversation with a relative who is learning to be an architect;

• reading and reporting on a book about the work of a famous scientist.

Third Grade

2 Describes some jobs of the past and how people did them.

As they begin to explore history, third graders can think about the kinds of jobs people did and what they needed to accomplish them, and make comparisons with jobs today. Third graders demonstrate this understanding by:

• writing up an interview with a senior citizen about running a pharmacy in the early 1900s;

• making drawings and paintings of how the early settlers constructed homes;

• making a model of a farm from the early 1900s;

• dramatizing scenes about how people long ago carried out daily chores.

Fourth Grade

No equivalent performance indicator at this level.

Fifth Grade

No equivalent performance indicator at this level.

V Social Studies

Kindergarten

3 Begins to be aware of technology and how it affects their lives.

Five year olds are very aware of the technology that is so much a part of the world around them (television, telephones, video games, VCRs, microwave ovens, computers). Often they are more adept at using computers and VCRs than many adults who did not grow up with this technology. Examples of how children show an understanding of how technology influences their life include:

• building machines with Legos, unit blocks or Tinker Toys;

• looking through a microscope to see "invisible" things;

• using the class computer to play a learning game;

• turning hollow blocks into a simulated rocket control center;

• pretending to take pictures with a Polaroid camera;

• beginning to use computers for word processing.

First Grade

3 Identifies some ways technology influences people's lives.

First graders can begin to recognize what constitutes a tool and how tools help us do things better. They can be expected to identify some forms of technology used in everyday life (cars, bridges, televisions, computers, stoves, VCRs) and describe some ways they affect our lives (communicating, crossing water, traveling long distances, watching TV, playing computer games). Examples include:

• sharing ideas in a group discussion about future means of communication;

• drawing and writing in a journal about computers;

• learning about an inventor at home and retelling the information to the class;

• constructing a complex highway system in the block area;

• creating an invention in the classroom using found materials;

• beginning to use the word processor for keeping records on science projects.

Second Grade

3 Identifies some ways technology influences people's lives.

Second graders can consider how technology affects people's jobs, leisure activities, and their knowledge of far-away places. They can be expected to describe some ways in which things people have designed (methods of communication, transportation, and information organization) make life easier or more difficult. Examples of how they do this include:

• reading a story about an inventor and telling the class about it;

• coming up with a problem and trying to invent a device to solve it;

• watching a video about how dams are constructed and then making a drawing of a dam;

• imagining life in their town before telephones were invented and writing a story about how local news was communicated;

• exploring multimedia effects in a science project on the computer.

Third Grade

3 Identifies some ways technology influences people's lives.

As third graders learn about how things have changed over time, they can reflect on how technology has changed and the ways these changes affect our lives. For example, as they think about what transportation was like in the past and compare it with the present, they can consider how such change affects people's jobs and leisure activities. Examples of how third graders express this understanding include:

• reading a biography of a famous inventor and making a presentation about it to the class;

• making a chart comparing current farm equipment to that of the past;

• making a drawing of the first television set or early computers and writing a report about it;

• making a list of all the machines in their house and marking those items that would not have been there a century ago;

• completing writing, math, and science work on the computer.

Fourth Grade

2 Shows some understanding of the historical interaction between people and technology.

Fourth graders can be expected to think about how technology has influenced people's lifestyles in the past and how it continues to do so today. They can then begin to analyze how technology has affected people in terms of jobs, economics, communications, and opportunities. Ways that nine year olds express this understanding include:

• using a classroom computer/modem to communicate with another student in another part of the country or world;

• writing a research report about current technology and tracing it back to its origins (computers, jets, cars);

• designing a possible future invention and writing about its potential significance to society;

• writing a skit based on the life of an inventor, including the impact that one invention had on society.

Fifth Grade

2 Shows understanding of the historical interaction between people and technology.

Fifth graders continue to develop understanding of how science and technology affects people's lives. They can reflect on how people in the past used materials to improve their standard of living and compare it to what occurs today. In making these comparisons, they can begin to consider the implications of technological advances on the future. Examples include:

• presenting information about how particular inventions affected society at the time they were created;

• creating inventions that might exist in the future and writing about their potential significance to society;

• making charts that compare tools used by an ancient culture (for example, for cooking, hunting, sewing) with those used today and describing how the users' lives differed because of them.

V Social Studies

V Social Studies

C Rights and responsibilities

Kindergarten	First Grade	Second Grade

Kindergarten

1 Recognizes the reasons for rules.

Children's understanding of the reasons for rules and laws comes about as they discuss problems in the classroom and school, and participate in making reasonable rules that directly involve them. Ways that children reveal their understanding of the need for rules include:

• helping to set the rules for the number of children playing at the sand table, and discussing why the rules were made and what could happen if the rules aren't followed;

• discussing and playing out the reasons for traffic rules, such as red and green traffic lights, solid and broken highway lines, stop signs, and the role of crossing guards, and police officers;

• exploring various family rules (What are some rules in each family? How many families have rules that are like rules in other families?);

• explaining classroom rules to a classmate;

• talking about school rules that apply to children in every classroom (for example, walking quietly in the hallways).

First Grade

1 Shows beginning understanding of why rules exist.

Children's understanding of the reasons for rules and laws comes about as they discuss everyday problems in the classroom and school, and participate in the formulation of reasonable rules. They can begin to learn that everyone wants to be treated fairly and that certain rules help make this possible. Gradually, they can consider how rules and laws help communities. Ways that children reveal this understanding include:

• helping to set classroom rules;

• mediating a conflict over a game rule;

• participating in group discussions (for example, considering why there are traffic and anti-shoplifting laws).

Second Grade

1 Shows beginning understanding of why rules exist.

Children's understanding of the reasons for rules and laws comes about as they discuss everyday problems in the classroom and school, and participate in the formulation of reasonable rules. Gradually they can consider how rules and laws are created, with the goal of helping to preserve people's rights. Ways that children reveal this understanding include:

• helping to set classroom rules;

• reacting to incidents of unfairness portrayed in stories;

• conducting a survey of children and adults about why laws should exist;

• helping a peer mediate a conflict.

Third Grade

1 Shows some understanding of how rules and laws help protect people and property.

Eight year olds' understanding of the reasons for rules and laws comes about as they discuss everyday problems in the classroom and school, and participate in the formulation of reasonable rules. They can consider some ways in which rules and laws protect people's rights and attempt to ensure that people are treated fairly. As they explore themes related to long ago, they can begin to compare how laws are made and upheld today as compared with earlier times. Some examples of how third graders express their understanding include:

• participating in group discussion about fair consequences;

• mediating a conflict over a game rule;

• writing in a journal about why communities need rules and laws to function;

• writing a research report about how laws were upheld in this country's early settlements;

• dramatizing a courtroom scene.

Fourth Grade

No equivalent performance indicator at this level.

Fifth Grade

No equivalent performance indicator at this level.

V Social Studies

V Social Studies

C Rights and responsibilities continued

Kindergarten

No equivalent performance indicator at this level.

First Grade

No equivalent performance indicator at this level.

Second Grade

No equivalent performance indicator at this level.

Third Grade

No equivalent performance indicator at this level.

Fourth Grade

1 Recognizes how individuals participate in society.

Nine year olds are eager to become more involved in decisions that affect their school lives. They want to know that their opinions are heard and that they play an important part in decision-making. They can be objective enough to understand that fair decisions might not always benefit them. The more meaningful experiences they have making decisions, the more motivated they are to be informed decision-makers. Examples of students demonstrating this skill include:

• creating a mock government (including an executive, legislative, and judicial component, and role playing real and/or simulated classroom issues);

• participating in classroom meetings that model democratic processes;

• problem-solving about relevant classroom and school problems;

• participating in student council.

Fifth Grade

1 Recognizes the ways individuals participate in society.

Ten year olds are ready to take on more active and sophisticated roles in the decision-making process within their school community. Current issues become more relevant to them as they learn how to engage in meaningful discussions and express their points of view. They can explore ways that people participate and contribute to society and make comparisons between past and present. Examples include:

• creating a mock government (including executive, legislative, and judicial components and role playing real or created classroom issues);

• participating in classroom meetings that model a democratic process;

• solving relevant classroom and school problems;

• discussing the role of government in social issues (homelessness, drugs, violence, war);

• showing empathy for the current or past struggles of humanity (people affected by earthquakes, the hardships experienced by immigrants coming to a new home, people's lack of basic necessities) and proposing governmental strategies to address these problems.

V Social Studies

Kindergarten

2 Recognizes reasons for leadership.

By the time children are five, they can begin to relate to the idea of leadership both in their classroom and in their community. They can see the important roles that the teacher and principal play in making things run in an orderly way. Five year olds can participate in assigning leadership roles for various class activities. Their understanding of leadership expands to the community as they identify the leaders in their community (the librarian, the mayor). Children show their beginning understanding of leadership roles by:

• playing teacher or fire chief in the dramatic play area;

• talking with peers about the job of a person "in charge" during snack or circle time;

• deciding to be the leader for the block building that will take place;

• making a book about the things that must be done by a particular leader in school or in the community.

First Grade

2 Recognizes the qualities of good leadership.

Six year olds have a beginning understanding of what it means to be a classroom leader. Learning about leaders in their community (principal, town council member, police chief) helps children consider the qualities of good leadership, how good leaders help groups function effectively, and how leaders are selected or elected. Children show their beginning understanding of leadership by:

• assuming positive leadership roles in games and projects;

• observing how a story character showed leadership qualities;

• sharing information from an interview with the principal;

• suggesting that a class vote determine the guinea pig's name.

Second Grade

2 Recognizes the characteristics of good leadership and fair decision-making.

Seven year olds have some understanding of what it means to be a classroom leader, and fair decision-making is very important to them. Seven year olds acquire this understanding best through classroom activities related to leadership and decision-making. As they learn about leaders in their community (principal, town council member, mayor) they can consider the qualities of good leadership, how good leaders help groups function effectively, how leaders are selected or elected, and how groups make decisions. They demonstrate their understanding of leadership by:

• suggesting that a vote settle a disagreement about which game to play;

• discussing how a story character showed leadership qualities;

• interviewing a local community leader and then reporting back to the class.

Third Grade

2 Shows beginning understanding of government functions.

Eight year olds continue to need time and practice learning what makes a good leader and how fair decisions are made. In addition to firsthand experiences in the classroom, third graders can find out about the basic structure and function of local government. By reading stories about historical times or other cultures, third graders can reflect on why different groups had different ways of handling decisions. Some ways third graders demonstrate their emerging understanding in this area include:

• describing how they would address a local issue if they were in an influential position;

• role-playing specific decision-making situations;

• doing research on how decisions were made in earlier times and presenting the information in writing or through drama;

• participating in student government.

Fourth Grade

2 Shows beginning understanding of the purposes and structures of governments.

Fourth graders' knowledge of government begins with understanding the rules that apply inside and outside their classrooms and then extend to the more complex government of laws and structures existing within and beyond their communities. They start to recognize the diverse needs of a society (caring for people, protecting resources) and begin to compare and contrast different kinds of governments (for example, past, present, foreign). Based on this emergent awareness, nine year olds begin to consider how decisions are made and enforced in society. Examples include:

• participating in class simulations that enact the functions of a democratic government (executive, legislative, and judicial);

• sharing a newspaper article that addresses current governmental issues and events (environmental legislation, government positions on human rights, elections);

• making a chart that compares and contrasts different forms of government.

Fifth Grade

2 Shows understanding of the purposes and structures of governments.

In the fifth grade, children are ready to study different kinds of governmental structures that exist throughout the world. They can consider the historical development of the country and the reasons that led to the shaping of the governmental structure. They can also explore how the values and attitudes of society are reflected in government. Examples include:

• researching the formation of several different military dictatorships and comparing the similarities and differences that led to that particular form of government;

• dramatizing scenes that depict historical political conflicts;

• participating in a small group discussion that focuses on how government policies benefit different parts of the population;

• writing a news article about a current government undergoing change;

• comparing various components of governmental structures in several countries (election process, leadership, judicial system) through a chart.

V Social Studies

D People and where they live

Kindergarten	First Grade	Second Grade

Kindergarten

1 Shows interest in how people affect the environment.

Five year old children are just beginning to consider the environment in more general and abstract ways. With teacher guidance and support, they can begin to look at the ways people take care of and hurt the world around them. Children show this beginning understanding by:

• recycling lunch containers and other paper products used during the day, and discussing what happens when these waste products are thrown in the trash bins;

• sharing with classmates and the teacher how trash gets scattered along the roadways and giving suggestions for ways that children can help with this problem;

• visiting a local pond or lake and talking about what they find, what belongs there, what has been left by people, and whether they like it or not;

• discussing ways to recycle paper and cans, and being interested in why this is important.

First Grade

1 Begins to recognize how people affect their environment.

At six, children can do projects and enter discussions that help them begin to understand the ways people use and abuse their environment. Children demonstrate their understanding through such concrete actions as:

• remembering to use classroom recycling bins;

• participating in discussions about environmental issues (for example, local recycling issues and water pollution);

• making references to environmental concerns in a journal entry or during puppet plays, skits, or dramatic play with blocks.

Second Grade

1 Recognizes how people affect their environment.

As seven year olds begin to become more aware of how people change their environment for specific purposes (such as building highways, cutting down trees, and burning coal), they can think about how these changes have both positive and negative effects. Some ways second graders demonstrate this understanding include:

• reminding classmates to use classroom recycling bins;

• expressing concern during class discussions about environmental issues (for example, recycling and water pollution);

• drawing pictures of how the town landscape might have looked at an earlier time, and explaining why it changed.

Third Grade

1 Recognizes how people affect their environment.

By the time children are eight years old, they can be expected to think about how people have changed the environment for specific purposes (such as building dams, bridges, highways, and skyscrapers). As they explore the positive and negative effects of these changes, they gain an awareness of how they can contribute to preserving the earth's natural resources. Examples of this understanding include:

• showing concern for pollution (participating in discussions, initiating a classroom recycling project, bringing in news articles about toxic waste in a local river);

• writing a research report about factories along the local river;

• writing an article for the school newspaper about recycling;

• looking for books in the library about a topic related to pollution.

Fourth Grade

1 Recognizes positive and negative ways that people affect their environment.

Fourth graders begin to understand how people use natural resources to satisfy societal needs (for example, oil drilling, farming, transportation, the creation of wildlife preserves). They begin to think critically about ways these methods have been both advantageous and destructive to the environment. Examples include:

• planning and implementing classroom or school-wide environmental programs (recycling, gardening, caring for animals);

• publishing an environmental newsletter;

• writing letters to officials about environmental concerns, and encouraging peers and adults to do so;

• writing research reports about local environmental problems.

Fifth Grade

1 Recognizes positive and negative ways that people affect their environment.

Most ten year olds are aware of current environmental issues that affect their local environment (for example, pollution, landfill needs, waste) or of problems that exist throughout the world (oil spills, deforestation, acid rain). They can critically analyze how the environment has been affected by human endeavors throughout history. Examples include:

• publishing an environmental newsletter that addresses a range of local issues;

• debating the pros and cons of building nuclear reactors, malls, or dams;

• writing to officials to express concern over local environmental problems or inviting community members to the school for project presentation;

• writing a research report comparing local environmental problems with those elsewhere in the world.

V Social Studies

D **People and where they live** continued

Kindergarten	First Grade	Second Grade
No equivalent performance indicator at this level.	2 **Begins to identify ways the environment affects how people live and work.**	2 **Identifies ways the environment affects how people live and work.**

First Grade, continued:

Six year olds are just beginning to make connections between how the climate and the physical features of their environment affect the way people live. For example, if children live in a cold climate, they have to dress warmly in the winter and their homes need heat. As six year olds study the kinds of work people do in the local community, they consider how jobs are affected by location (for example, the need for special clothing or vehicles during certain seasons). Some ways children reveal this geographic understanding include:

• constructing models that detail the local environment;

• drawing or painting pictures that reflect an understanding of the community's physical features;

• offering a logical explanation during a group discussion about why many community jobs are related to snow removal or hurricane protection.

Second Grade, continued:

When seven year olds make connections between how the climate and physical features of their environment affect the way people live (such as jobs, clothing, housing, foods), they are engaged in geographical thinking. For example, if children live near a major body of water, they are likely to be acquainted with many different jobs related to shipping and/or tourism. Some ways children reveal this understanding include:

• constructing models, drawing pictures or making paintings that detail the local environment;

• writing research reports (for example, about transportation or jobs in the community);

• participating in group discussions about the way their community's life has been shaped by the environment.

Third Grade

2 Identifies ways the environment affects how people live and work.

When eight year olds consider the ways people's lives are affected by their environment (for example, climate and physical features), they are engaged in geographical thinking. Whether studying the local community or a place far away or long ago, children this age can consider how these factors may, for example, influence housing, transportation, foods, or jobs. Ways that children reveal this understanding include:

• constructing models, drawing pictures, or making paintings that detail the physical environment and its relationship to people's daily lives;

• writing a story about a desert-dwelling family;

• writing a research report about the houses in a bayou;

• observing how a story's action is determined by the physical environment;

• recognizing differences in wheelchair accessibility in warm and cold climates.

Fourth Grade

2 Shows an understanding of how environmental factors shape people's lives.

Nine year olds are developing an awareness of how resources, climate, and land forms affect people's lives. They begin to describe how people, in the present and the past, meet their needs for jobs, food, shelter, water, and security by using elements of the environment. Some ways students demonstrate this understanding include:

• constructing models, drawing pictures, or making paintings that highlight landscape features;

• writing a story that includes information about the effect of the environment on its inhabitants;

• comparing and contrasting how environmental factors in two regions influence people's occupations.

Fifth Grade

2 Shows an understanding of how environmental factors shape people's lives.

Ten year olds have an understanding of the impact of resources, geographic features, and climatic patterns on people's lives. Building on their knowledge of economics, science, and technology, they can be expected to consider how the environmental factors of particular regions influence people's quality of life (job opportunities, transportation, food, shelter). Some ways students reveal this understanding include:

• constructing models, drawing pictures, or making paintings that include details about the physical environment and its relationship to people based on research about a culture in the past;

• writing a story that includes information about the effect of an environment on its inhabitants;

• creating a model of an imaginary human settlement that includes climate, physical features, resources, crops, clothing and other elements, and describing the lifestyle of the people.

V Social Studies

V Social Studies

D People and where they live continued

Kindergarten

2 Expresses beginning geographic thinking.

Five year olds can begin to understand the geographic relationship of their homes to school and to friends' houses. They can begin to understand their own classroom map. They show their ability to think geographically by:

• building a familiar street with blocks and positioning homes and stores in proper order;

• drawing a map of the classroom, showing the windows, tables, and activity and interest areas;

• describing what they see and pass on their way home from school;

• drawing a map or diagram of their bedroom;

• using a flannel board to show the location of objects in a room;

• using building blocks to show how the playground looks.

First Grade

3 Shows beginning understanding that maps represent actual places.

For six year olds, learning that real places can be represented symbolically occurs as children make drawings, build with blocks, and create models of real places (for example, drawing a map of the classroom, or creating a model of the neighborhood with milk cartons). Creating and reading pictorial maps helps six year olds become increasingly familiar with symbolic representation. Some ways children demonstrate this understanding include:

• constructing a block building of the movie theater and finding techniques to replicate details (such as the screen, seats, snack bar, and ticket booth);

• making a blueprint of a block structure;

• making a map of the playground;

• drawing a treasure map.

Second Grade

3 Recognizes that maps represent actual places, and uses simple mapping skills.

Children this age develop mapping skills by making concrete representations (drawn maps and 3-D models) of actual places they have seen firsthand. As they come to understand that maps are symbolic representations of real places, they can learn about other mapping symbols. At seven, children demonstrate their understanding of maps by:

• constructing block buildings and including details that replicate actual objects (bridges, tunnels, roads);

• making maps (of their classroom, bedroom, or playground) and labeling them;

• representing through drawings and words the route taken from home to school;

• experimenting with using symbols to represent real places on a map and creating a key;

• locating an important place on a world map or globe (for example, where a grandparent was born or where a folk tale takes place).

Third Grade

3 Reads and makes simple maps.

As eight year olds become increasingly able to think symbolically, they can progress from simply creating concrete representations (drawn maps and 3-D models) of actual places they have seen first-hand to making models and maps of places they have not seen (including imaginary ones). They can also begin to interpret information on real maps. Children demonstrate their understanding of maps by:

• constructing models (for example, of communities or cities);

• making maps and using symbols (of the local environment, imaginary places, or story settings);

• making models that express geographical features (rivers, mountains);

• using globes, atlases, and maps as resources;

• drawing aerial representations of a town, city, or state.

Fourth Grade

3 Reads and constructs maps.

By fourth grade, children understand that maps are representations of real places. They should be able to interpret different types of maps, as well as create different representations of geographical features. They are intrigued by distant places and historical time periods. Their developing ability to think abstractly means they can use symbols to represent things they have never seen. Examples include:

• constructing models (of communities, regions, cities) that express geographical relationships;

• using globes, atlases, photographs, books, or flat maps as resources;

• measuring lengths and distances on maps using a scale bar;

• comparing maps (for purpose, content, style, usefulness, clarity, and accuracy);

• using a map index with a map grid.

Fifth Grade

3 Reads, interprets, and constructs a variety of maps.

Fifth graders further develop their geographic thinking through making, reading, and interpreting maps. They can use maps to hypothesize and draw conclusions about historical events. Examples of their understanding include:

• exploring early settlements and economic development by interpreting maps;

• constructing models (of communities, regions, cities) that express geographical relationships;

• using globes, atlases, photographs, books, or flat maps as resources;

• comparing maps (for purpose, content, style, usefulness, clarity, and accuracy).

V Social Studies

Kindergarten	First Grade	Second Grade
No equivalent performance indicator at this level.	**1 Shows beginning understanding of time and how the past influences people's lives.**	**1 Shows beginning understanding of time and how the past influences people's lives.**

First Grade

1 Shows beginning understanding of time and how the past influences people's lives.

First graders learn about time by exploring clock and calendar time. By reflecting on their own histories, they begin to learn about chronological time. Some ways children express this emerging understanding include:

• drawing and writing in a journal about a memory from preschool or kindergarten;

• making a timeline of their first six years of life;

• bringing personal objects from the past to share with classmates (such as a quilt, a photo album, or a favorite but outgrown toy);

• telling a personal anecdote about the past in response to hearing something read aloud.

Second Grade

1 Shows beginning understanding of time and how the past influences people's lives.

Second graders continue to learn about time by exploring clock and calendar time. By reflecting on their own histories, they acquire an understanding of chronological time and can consider some ways that the past affects what they are doing now. Conversations and interviews with older relatives can extend children's thinking about the past. Some ways seven year olds express their understanding include:

• writing a story based on a personal memory;

• making a timeline of their first seven years of life;

• writing an autobiography;

• making a pictorial timeline of a parent's or grandparent's life.

Third Grade

1 Shows understanding of time and how the past influences people's lives.

When eight year olds explore their own history and that of members of their families, by conducting interviews and studying photographs, they begin to think about cause and effect relationships (such as, "Why did this happen in this way?", "What would have happened?", and "What might happen in the future?"). Direct experience with the past helps children prepare for more expansive thinking about history. Some ways they show their growing understanding of how the past shapes the present and the future include:

• making personal timelines;

• dramatizing situations from the past;

• finding books that relate to a discovery made while interviewing an older relative;

• writing a story based on memories.

Fourth Grade

No equivalent performance indicator at this level.

Fifth Grade

No equivalent performance indicator at this level.

The Arts

The emphasis in this domain is on children's engagement with the arts (dance, dramatics, music, and art), both actively and receptively. The components address how children use the arts to express, represent, and integrate their experiences, ideas, and emotions, and how children develop an appreciation for the arts. This domain does not emphasize mastery of skills related to particular art forms. Rather, it focuses on how using and appreciating the arts enables children to demonstrate what they know and to expand their thinking.

VI The Arts

A Expression and representation

Kindergarten

1 Uses a variety of art materials to explore and express ideas and emotions.

Five year olds become comfortable using a variety of media and enhance their sense of mastery and creativity through experience with art materials. They begin to express feelings and ideas through their art work, in addition to expressing them verbally. Examples of exploration and expression with art materials include:

• trying a variety of expressive media (markers, brush and finger painting, printing, collage, play dough, clay);

• using one medium for a period of time to develop greater control and expertise;

• drawing or painting the way they feel when happy;

• making a book with their own pictures to illustrate a story they dictated;

• creating an object or animal with clay.

First Grade

1 Uses the arts to express and represent ideas, experiences, and emotions.

Six year olds can make detailed representations of ideas, experiences, and emotions, but they tend to do this spontaneously. Examples of ways children demonstrate this include:

• creating a visual representation of an object, place, or event (for example, painting a picture of the firehouse after a class visit, or constructing a model bridge using straws, popsicle sticks, cardboard, and aluminum foil);

• creating architectural structures using blocks, Legos, or other building materials;

• using musical instruments to express an interpretation of a story or poem;

• acting out a scene or role based on a story recently read aloud by the teacher.

Second Grade

1 Uses the arts to express and represent ideas, experiences, and emotions.

Seven year olds can plan increasingly detailed representations of ideas, experiences, and emotions. Their representations may be more complex, because they are able to retain several details about each experience. Examples of how children demonstrate these abilities include:

• creating a visual representation of an object, place, or event (for example, painting a self-portrait or creating an animal with clay);

• creating increasingly intricate architectural structures using blocks, Legos, and other building materials;

• using musical instruments to express an interpretation of a story or poem;

• dramatizing a scene from a story.

Third Grade

1 Uses the arts to express and represent ideas, experiences, and emotions.

Eight year olds can plan and organize detailed representations of ideas, experiences, and emotions. Their representations are more complex because they are able to utilize many details of ideas and experiences. Examples of how children demonstrate these abilities include:

• creating a visual or physical representation of an object, place, or event (for example, constructing a model, painting a mural, or creating an intricate collage);

• creating complicated architectural structures using building materials;

• composing songs or using musical instruments that relate to a thematic study;

• dramatizing a story.

Fourth Grade

1 Uses the arts to express and represent ideas, experiences, and emotions.

Through art, children can be observers, inquirers, and learners. As children integrate artistic experiences into other subject areas, they are able to delve deeper into the topics being studied, which enriches their artwork. Examples of this include:

• creating a visual representation of an object, place, or event (for example, model, mural, collage) related to classroom themes and studies;

• learning crafts from other cultures;

• dramatizing mythical or historical characters and events (taking on the personality of gods and goddesses from Ancient Egypt or the pioneers during Westward Expansion);

• drawing what they have observed with accurate detail and color;

• recording stories on audiotapes with sound effects, instruments, and narration;

• performing a musical composition they have learned.

Fifth Grade

1 Uses the arts to express and represent ideas, experiences, and emotions.

Students at this age can explore sophisticated means of artistic expression. Because they are able to retain ideas and experiences, their representations are more accurate and detailed. Examples of ways students demonstrate these abilities include:

• creating visual representations of objects, places, or events (model, mural, collage) related to classroom themes and studies;

• composing songs or using musical instruments as part of a musical study;

• retelling or dramatizing stories from other cultures;

• exploring a craft in depth;

• creating partner dances based on traditional dance figures.

VI The Arts

A Expression and representation continued

Kindergarten

2 Participates in group music experiences.

Five year olds are able to master the use of simple instruments, such as rhythm sticks, tambourines or drums. They are interested in the sounds that more complicated instruments (piano, guitar) make, and in how they are played. They enjoy singing time, making up silly and rhyming verses, learning finger plays, and using music to tell stories and express feelings. Often, they will make up songs to accompany other activities, such as when swinging outside, or putting on their outside clothes. Examples of music participation include:

• exploring musical instruments that are in the classroom;

• joining singing times;

• clapping to the beat of a song or tape;

• using musical instruments to create a mood to go along with a puppet show or a creative dance;

• combining music and movement to express a new feeling;

• composing their own songs, singing as they perform classroom routines, wait in line, or use the swings.

First Grade

2 Experiments with new ideas, materials, and activities in the arts.

Familiarity and experience contribute to children's ability to use art media with flexibility and inventiveness. For first graders, examples of this include:

• finding innovative ways to use collage and construction materials to build a realistic model of the inside of a house (rug samples, Styrofoam, pieces of wood, wallpaper samples);

• using many different materials to create detailed puppets and puppet show scenery;

• creating intricate mosaic designs using pattern blocks or other manipulatives;

• using several musical instruments to create puppet show sound effects.

Second Grade

2 Experiments with new ideas, materials, and activities in the arts.

Familiarity and experience help children use art media with flexibility and inventiveness. For second graders, examples of this include:

• creating sculptures using found materials;

• using paints and brushes in experimental ways to create texture in a painting;

• using a variety of musical instruments to create puppet show sound effects;

• making up a new verse for a song.

Third Grade

2 Experiments with new ideas, materials, and activities in the arts.

Familiarity and experience help children use art media with flexibility and inventiveness. For third graders, examples include:

• using body movements, voice, and props to create a vivid, dramatic interpretation of a scene from a book;

• mixing paints to create many colors to paint a realistic forest scene;

• experimenting with tempo and volume in a musical composition;

• hearing a song and making up a new series of verses.

Fourth Grade

2 Experiments with new ideas, materials, and activities in the arts.

Children grow artistically by exploring a variety of more sophisticated materials and techniques. Their developing intellectual abilities allow them to create novel combinations and uses for materials, solve problems, and analyze new artistic experiences. Examples include:

• exploring multi-cultural arts (traditional folktales from another culture, Caribbean music, Aboriginal dream maps);

• working with more complex art materials and processes (oil paint, linoleum and other carving tools, copper tooling, detailed stitchery);

• making up verses to a song based on a well-known melody or chorus;

• creating an original dance;

• responding to narration as a guide to create movement with sound (for example, becoming part of a machine);

• improvising with their voice or musical instruments;

• building models of imaginary places with realistic detail.

Fifth Grade

2 Experiments with new ideas, materials, and activities in the arts.

For some ten year olds, the performing arts enables them to express themselves in new ways. For others participating in the arts is difficult because their self-consciousness impedes their self-expression. Sometimes, ten year olds are more successful with visual arts that are structured and intellectually challenging. Their more refined motor skills, combined with abilities such as depicting objects more realistically, enable them to express themselves in a less self-conscious manner. Examples include:

• solving more complex design problems (figures drawn more in proportion or shading to show form);

• composing an original song or dance;

• participating in two- or three-part rounds;

• handling more complex art materials and processes (oil paint, linoleum and other carving tools, copper tooling, detailed stitchery);

• showing spatial effects through overlapping, depicting distant objects as smaller and farther up, and using a horizon line to show where land and sky meet.

A Expression and representation continued

Kindergarten	First Grade	Second Grade
3 Participates in and enjoys creative movement, dance, and drama.	**No equivalent performance indicator at this level.**	**No equivalent performance indicator at this level.**

Five year olds are very active and need opportunities to move and stretch their bodies. They are in constant motion, wiggling, changing positions, sitting in a variety of ways. They can harness this energy into creative and descriptive expressions of feelings and experiences through movement, dance, and drama. Examples include:

• participating in a group movement experience, suggesting ways to move, suggesting animals to imitate;

• planning or joining with others in the dramatization of a book or the retelling of a class event;

• creating a movement that responds to the beat of a record, or interpreting the mood conveyed by a classical composition;

• dramatizing a story they have created;

• creating a drama about something they are studying or have visited, such as a circus or a trip to the zoo.

Third Grade

No equivalent performance indicator at this level.

Fourth Grade

No equivalent performance indicator at this level.

Fifth Grade

No equivalent performance indicator at this level.

VI The Arts

B Artistic appreciation

Kindergarten	First Grade	Second Grade

Kindergarten

1 Shows interest in the work of others.

Many children express their interest in the arts as observers rather than as producers. Five year olds are able to appreciate the art of others, the skill of a dancer, or the ability to play an instrument. Some ways that children express this interest include:

• watching as classmates perform a puppet show or a dance they have created;

• listening to music tapes or records during choice time, indicating involvement by body language and facial expression;

• listening with attention and pleasure to a visiting artist, such as a poet, writer, musician, or magician;

• looking at illustrations in a book and appreciating the skill or beauty of the drawings;

• commenting with enthusiasm on the construction, artwork, or writing that classmates have produced.

First Grade

1 Shows interest in the work of others.

Many children express their interest in the arts as observers rather than as producers. Some ways children demonstrate their interest include:

• joining singing activities at a school assembly, and learning the words and songs;

• listening with pleasure to records, tapes, and live musical performances;

• showing interest in book illustrations.

Second Grade

1 Shows interest in the work of others.

Many children express their interest in the arts as observers rather than as producers. Some ways children demonstrate their interest include:

• joining in and learning the words to songs;

• listening with pleasure to records, tapes, and live musical performances;

• showing interest in book illustrations;

• being attentive during classroom presentations (sharing skits, artwork, and other creations).

Third Grade

1 Shows interest in the work of others.

Many children express their interest in the arts as observers rather than as producers. Some ways children demonstrate their interest include:

• joining in and learning the words of a song;

• listening with pleasure to records, tapes, and live musical performances;

• showing interest in book illustrations;

• being attentive during classroom presentations (sharing skits, artwork, and other creations).

Fourth Grade

1 Shows interest in the work of others.

Along with constructing a work of art and participating in the artistic process, students at this age practice criticism of their own work, and that of their peers and even accomplished artists. They are learning to articulate an intuitive and intellectual appreciation of art and performance. Examples of this include:

• taking time to admire and appreciate art displays throughout the school;

• exhibiting attentive and responsive behaviors during performances and asking follow-up questions in discussions after performances;

• writing personal responses to performances;

• responding to a famous piece of artwork by commenting on the artist's style and technique.

Fifth Grade

1 Shows interest in the work of others.

Along with constructing works of art, students at this age practice criticism of their own work, as well as the work of their peers and accomplished artists. Fifth graders can learn to appreciate performance and works of art. Examples of this include:

• responding to a famous piece of artwork by commenting on the artist's intention, style, technique, and message;

• recognizing and encouraging other student's abilities;

• expressing, identifying, and interpreting themes, concepts, and moods in various works of art;

• researching a musical or artistic subject (for example, art or music in different cultures, origins of artistic styles [Greek architecture, African masks, Egyptian hieroglyphics], and musical styles [classical, bee-bop, rock'n'roll]).

VI The Arts

B Artistic appreciation continued

Kindergarten	First Grade	Second Grade

Kindergarten

No equivalent performance indicator at this level.

First Grade

2 Interprets and extracts meaning from artistic products and experiences.

When children have opportunities to use and observe various art forms, they can begin to think about the meaning and interpretation of artistic products and experiences. Ways children do this include:

• recognizing that an illustration used colors to convey ideas and emotions;

• hearing music and relating it to real sounds (of animals, cars, machines);

• noticing that an actor's movements can convey ideas and emotions (such as age or happiness).

Second Grade

2 Interprets and extracts meaning from artistic products and experiences.

When children have opportunities to use and observe various art forms, they begin to think about the meaning and interpretation of artistic products and experiences. Ways children do this include:

• recognizing that an illustration used color, line, and shape to convey ideas and emotions;

• hearing music and relating it to real sounds (of animals, cars, machines);

• noticing that an actor's movements can convey ideas and emotions (such as age or happiness).

Third Grade

2 Interprets and extracts meaning from artistic products and experiences.

When children have opportunities to use and observe various art forms, they begin to think about the meaning and interpretation of artistic products and experiences. Ways children do this include:

• recognizing that an illustration used color, line, and shape to convey ideas and emotions;

• hearing music and relating it to real sounds (of animals, cars, machines);

• noticing that an actor's (child or adult) movements can convey ideas and emotions (such as age or happiness);

• representing an artistic experience using a different medium (for example, painting a picture that represents feelings expressed in music).

Fourth Grade

2 Interprets and extracts meaning from artistic products and experiences.

Students begin to recognize that a work of art is often a result of the artist making intentional choices to convey certain feelings or messages. Examples include:

• describing ways an artist used various techniques to convey an idea or emotion;

• listening to music and comparing or relating it to personal experiences;

• responding to music through interpretive movement;

• recognizing how an actor can give life to a fictional character.

Fifth Grade

2 Interprets and extracts meaning from artistic products and experiences.

Students begin to recognize that a work of art is often the result of the artist making intentional choices to convey a certain feeling or message . Some examples of this include:

• recognizing that an artist's drawing used color, line, shape, texture, and/or contrast to convey ideas and emotions;

• identifying a theme, mood, or feeling in a piece of instrumental music;

• writing personal responses to artistic experiences.

VII

Physical Development

The emphasis in this domain is on physical development as an integral part of children's well-being and ability to take advantage of educational opportunities. The components address gross motor skills, fine motor skills, and personal health and safety. A principal focus is on children's ability to move in ways that demonstrate control, balance, and coordination. Fine motor skills are equally important in laying the groundwork for artistic expression, handwriting, and self-care skills. The third component addresses children's growing ability to understand and manage their personal health and safety.

VII Physical Development

A Gross motor development

Kindergarten	First Grade	Second Grade
1 Uses balance and control to perform large motor tasks.	**1 Moves with balance and control.**	**1 Moves with agility, balance, and control.**

Kindergarten

1 Uses balance and control to perform large motor tasks.

Five year olds are very active, seeming to be in constant motion. They are still developing control over their bodies and are practicing movement skills. Some ways that children show their growing balance and control include:

• hopping on each foot;

• moving confidently and safely around the room, in the halls, and when going up and down stairs;

• walking up or down stairs while holding an object in one or both hands;

• carrying a glass of water or juice across the room without spilling it.

First Grade

1 Moves with balance and control.

Six year olds tend to be active, although sometimes rather clumsy. They are continuing to develop their balance and the control of their gross motor tasks. Examples of how they demonstrate these skills include:

• walking across the cafeteria carrying a lunch tray without mishap;

• distributing materials (books, papers, art materials) in the classroom without dropping them;

• playing on outdoor equipment with ease (such as climbers and swings).

Second Grade

1 Moves with agility, balance, and control.

As seven year olds develop more balance and control, they can move with greater speed, accuracy, and agility in many different activities. Examples of how they demonstrate increasing balance and control include:

• walking with free, sure steps and moving easily through the classroom and hallways;

• distributing materials (books, papers, art materials) in the classroom without dropping them;

• running easily with the ability to swerve, dodge, and change directions suddenly.

Third Grade

1 **Moves with agility, speed, and coordination while performing complex tasks.**

Because the energy level of eight year olds is high, they move around a great deal. Moving with greater speed, accuracy, and agility in many different activities is typical of eight year olds. Some ways they demonstrate this include:

• moving furniture easily in the classroom in order to make room for special activities (a skit, game, or movement activity);

• running easily with the ability to swerve, dodge, and change directions suddenly in tag games;

• learning a series of jump rope tricks and combining them into a routine;

• running and kicking a ball.

Fourth Grade

1 **Moves with increasing agility, speed, and coordination while performing complex tasks.**

Nine year olds have an increased ability to move with balance, coordination, and control. Their developing muscular strength, endurance, and flexibility enable them to perform more sophisticated tasks. Examples include:

• running easily and being able to swerve, dodge, and change directions suddenly when involved in a game;

• learning a series of jump-rope tricks and combining them into a routine;

• practicing a series of tumbling and balancing acts with control;

• rearranging chairs, tables, and desks when classroom activities require additional space.

Fifth Grade

1 **Moves with increasing agility, speed, and coordination while performing complex tasks.**

As ten year olds improve their ability to move with balance, coordination, and control, they gain confidence in their overall performance. Their muscular strength, endurance, and flexibility allow them to use their bodies in increasingly sophisticated ways. Examples include:

• running and throwing a variety of objects with accuracy and distance (for example, frisbees, a variety of balls, rings);

• running easily and being able to swerve, dodge, and change directions suddenly when involved in a game;

• manipulating a jump rope in different patterns while creating a routine;

• rearranging chairs, tables, and desks when classroom activities require additional space.

VII Physical Development

A Gross motor development continued

Kindergarten

2 Coordinates movements to perform tasks.

Five year olds are busy experimenting with how their bodies move. They are ready to combine various independent skills to accomplish new feats and meet new challenges. These include:

• skipping smoothly, alternating feet;

• walking, galloping, jumping, and running in rhythm to simple tunes and music patterns;

• climbing a slide ladder or using arms and feet together on the jungle gym;

• moving their body into position to catch a ball and throwing it in the right direction;

• building complex structures with hollow blocks and unit blocks (tall buildings, bridges, car repair garage, or a fire station).

First Grade

2 Coordinates movements to perform tasks.

Most six year olds are developing the ability to move with coordination in planned and skillful ways that involve combining several kinds of simultaneous movements. Examples of this include:

• jumping and turning a rope at the same time;

• throwing and catching a ball;

• running and then kicking a soccer ball.

Second Grade

2 Coordinates movements to perform complex tasks.

Most seven year olds can move with coordination in planned and skillful ways that involve several kinds of simultaneous movements. Examples include:

• combining several moves while jumping rope;

• completing a series of tumbling acts (such as somersaults and cartwheels);

• playing ball games that require coordination (tether ball, four-square, kickball);

• performing simple dance steps while using rhythm instruments.

Third Grade

2 Demonstrates coordinated movements in games, sports, and other activities.

Eight year olds are developing the ability to integrate their physical skills into sports, gymnastics, and dance. Examples include:

• performing a series of tumbling maneuvers (such as cartwheels and flips);

• running and then kicking a soccer ball during a game;

• swinging a bat and hitting a ball;

• performing intricate dance steps;

• throwing and catching a ball in skillful ways (in a softball game, when playing dodgeball, etc.).

Fourth Grade

2 Applies gross motor skills in games, sports, and other physical activities.

Fourth graders are learning to integrate their physical skills into more complex sports, gymnastics, and dance. Working in partnership or on a team requires students to integrate many skills simultaneously. Dribbling a basketball becomes more challenging when one is participating with others and must manage not only physical but social and emotional issues. Examples of students applying gross motor skills in physical activities include:

• throwing, catching, and kicking in a game;

• dribbling a ball with a small group during soccer or basketball practices;

• problem-solving through teamwork that involves physical movement.

Fifth Grade

2 Applies gross motor skills in games, sports, and other physical activities.

Fifth graders continue to integrate their physical skills into more complex sports, dance, and gymnastics. Working in partnerships or on teams requires students to integrate many skills simultaneously. Dribbling a basketball becomes more challenging when one is participating with others and must manage not only physical but social and emotional issues. Examples of this skill include:

• throwing, catching, and kicking during a game;

• dribbling a ball with hands and feet while preventing opponents from stealing the ball;

• playing games in small groups and using basic offensive and defensive strategies (throwing, kicking, or dribbling a ball);

• performing international, ethnic, historical or contemporary dances, games, and sports.

VII Physical Development

B Fine motor development

Kindergarten

1 Uses strength and control to accomplish fine motor tasks.

Five year olds are becoming very adept at using their small muscles to accomplish tasks. They can use their fingers and arms to accomplish certain tasks much more easily than a year ago. Since some children are more skillful than others, it is important to look for growth rather than specific accomplishments at this age of transition. Some skills to look for include:

• tearing a piece of tape off a roll of tape;

• using a stapler to join several pages;

• using a paper punch without help;

• using scissors successfully;

• making more complicated forms with the geoboard;

• hammering two pieces of wood together to make an airplane.

First Grade

1 Uses strength and control to accomplish tasks.

As six year olds develop more strength and control in their hands and wrists, they become increasingly able to use materials with precision. Some ways they demonstrate this are:

• using scissors to cut out an outlined figure;

• placing blocks on a structure without knocking it down;

• using a stapler to join several pages of a story.

Second Grade

1 Uses strength and control to accomplish tasks.

By seven, children have increased strength and dexterity in their fingers, hands, and wrists. This enables them to perform more-precise fine motor tasks. Some examples include:

• using a stapler or hole punch effectively;

• using scissors to cut straight and curved lines, and shapes;

• working with woodworking tools;

• using the computer keyboard easily.

Third Grade

1 **Uses strength, control, and eye-hand coordination to accomplish tasks.**

Eight year olds have increased dexterity and eye-hand coordination, enabling them to perform several fine motor tasks in an organized way. Examples of this include:

• using woodworking tools to complete a project;

• playing a computer game that requires speed and accuracy;

• creating a beadwork pattern using a needle, string, and beads;

• using tweezers to prepare a microscope slide (for example, placing a fish scale or insect part on a slide);

• threading a needle.

Fourth Grade

1 **Combines and organizes several fine motor skills to produce a product independently.**

Most nine year olds want their work to look sophisticated and realistic. Much of their work involves numerous steps that require combining several fine motor skills with some degree of precision. Fourth graders can be expected to work independently although they may need help when a project becomes too challenging. Examples include:

• building a model out of a variety of materials related to a thematic study (a house from a country studied, bird of prey, ecosystem);

• creating model costumes that include sewing and stenciling;

• writing legibly in cursive style with proper spacing;

• cutting accurately with linoleum cutters during art projects;

• using a variety of carving and cutting tools to create three-dimensional maps;

• painting or drawing a design or picture with small details.

Fifth Grade

1 **Combines and organizes several fine motor skills to produce a product independently.**

Fifth graders can engage in activities that require detail and precision and make products of greater sophistication and realism. Frequently this involves numerous steps that require several fine motor skills at varying levels and may require guidance from peers or adults. Some ways a fifth grader might demonstrate this understanding include:

• creating costumes that involve sewing and stenciling;

• using a variety of materials to create three-dimensional models (for example, wood, clay, and soap for sculpting, and yarn, reeds, grasses for weaving);

• measuring and drawing straight lines with rulers, yardsticks, and surveying tape;

• creating three-dimensional, paper shapes (platonic solids).

VII Physical Development

B Fine motor development continued

Kindergarten	First Grade	Second Grade
2 Uses eye-hand coordination to perform fine motor tasks.	**2 Uses eye-hand coordination to perform tasks.**	**2 Uses eye-hand coordination to perform tasks.**

Kindergarten

2 Uses eye-hand coordination to perform fine motor tasks.

Five year olds are continuing to improve their eye-hand coordination. They enjoy playing with manipulatives and blocks, and sometimes work with a finished product in mind. Five year olds demonstrate eye-hand coordination by:

• putting together 18- to 25-piece puzzles using picture as well as shape clues;

• building specific block structures from a model without knocking the structures down;

• constructing planned projects out of Legos, Bristle Blocks, table blocks, and Tinker Toys;

• cutting more accurately on a straight line or around pictures;

• cutting fabric into shapes to use for collage;

• using tape, scissors, and the stapler to create 3-D objects, such as a house or an airplane;

• dressing in a variety of costumes in the dramatic play area (buttoning shirts, zipping jackets).

First Grade

2 Uses eye-hand coordination to perform tasks.

The increasing eye-hand coordination of six year olds enables them to complete fine motor tasks when only one type of movement is involved. Combining several movements sometimes leads to frustration. Some examples of how they demonstrate eye-hand coordination includes:

• sewing clothing on a puppet;

• fitting pattern blocks and tangrams into pre-drawn outlines;

• striking the keys of a calculator, computer game, or keyboard with increasing accuracy.

Second Grade

2 Uses eye-hand coordination to perform tasks.

The increasing eye-hand coordination of seven year olds is often shown in work that requires more precise efforts (such as when writing with small letters, or when including more details in their drawings). They can combine several fine motor skills in an organized way to produce a product. Examples include:

• stringing bead patterns on yarn or thread;

• attaching pieces of cardboard together with masking tape to create a 3-D object;

• using a computer keyboard with increasing accuracy when writing a story.

Third Grade

No equivalent performance indicator at this level.

Fourth Grade

No equivalent performance indicator at this level.

Fifth Grade

No equivalent performance indicator at this level.

B Fine motor development continued

Kindergarten	First Grade	Second Grade

Kindergarten

3 Uses writing and drawing tools with some confidence and control.

Five year old children show increasing ability to use a variety of writing, drawing, and art tools. As their pencil grasp becomes established, some show interest in the rudimentary formation of letters, and repeatedly practice writing their name. At this age, children demonstrate their control of writing tools by:

• drawing pictures and designs with pencils, pens, and markers;

• using a pencil with their preferred hand while holding the paper in position with the other hand;

• using paints and brushes to form letters and symbols or to make repeating patterns.

First Grade

3 Uses writing and drawing tools with some control.

Most six year olds enjoy experimenting with writing and drawing. They often have difficulty keeping letters on a line when writing. Some ways that six year olds show they are developing necessary handwriting skills are:

• holding pencils, crayons, and markers with increasing ease;

• forming letters and numbers with greater accuracy;

• using one hand to write and the other to hold the paper.

Second Grade

3 Uses writing and drawing tools with some confidence and control.

By seven, most children can form letters and numbers easily, and can control their placement on a page. Some ways that seven year olds show increasing handwriting skills are:

• using crayons, markers, and paint brushes to create representational images;

• forming upper and lower case letters with accuracy;

• beginning to develop a handwriting style (such as forming certain letters in a particular way).

Third Grade

2 Uses writing tools with confidence and control.

Children of this age have better control of handwriting and are developing a personal style. Their often sloppy, informal handwriting is the result of their tendency to rush. When they take the time to write slowly, their handwriting is most likely to be clear and legible. Examples include:

• using writing tools with increasing ease for a purpose (such as writing stories, lists, letters, and charts);

• writing legibly with good spacing;

• beginning to use cursive writing;

• using various art media with confidence and control.

Fourth Grade

2 Uses tools with coordination and control.

Fourth graders can be expected to use familiar tools independently. Because they want their work to look sophisticated, they use tools with fine, sharp points to provide the increased accuracy they value. Examples of how fourth graders use tools include:

• using eye droppers, measuring utensils, or timing devices during a scientific investigation;

• using a compass to solve a math problem or while working on an art project;

• using woodworking tools to construct a model;

• playing musical instruments (piano, trumpet, guitar) with control;

• using keyboarding skills effectively for word processing and playing games.

Fifth Grade

2 Uses tools and materials with confidence and control.

By ten years of age, most children have many refined motor skills that enable them to work with a variety of tools. As they have opportunities to use different tools, they develop greater fine motor control, increase their confidence with tools, and become more responsible in tool use. Examples include:

• using protractors and compasses (to draw and measure angles and circles);

• using tools during an investigation (dissection tools, microscopes, eye droppers, scales, thermometers, measuring utensils);

• using calligraphy pens or X-acto knives to create artwork;

• writing legibly in cursive style;

• cutting detailed shapes for collages.

VII Physical Development

VII Physical Development

C Personal health and safety

Kindergarten

1 Performs self-care tasks competently.

Five year olds are quite competent about taking care of their own physical needs and often help classmates who are struggling with buttons and laces. They take pride in their skills and will often practice zipping jackets and tying bows just for the pleasure of doing it. They demonstrate competence by:

• taking care of their own toilet needs, asking for help with suspenders or other difficult clothing;

• putting on their own outdoor clothing with very little help and few reminders;

• pouring juice easily and without spills for snack or lunch;

• cleaning up art projects or other messy activities with relative skill;

• keeping track of their personal belongings and taking responsibility for keeping them safe;

• spreading peanut butter and doing other simple tasks with food.

First Grade

1 Shows beginning understanding of how to maintain physical health and well-being.

The first step in keeping oneself healthy and safe is knowing what the body needs to function properly: regular toilet use and other personal hygiene, nutritious food at regular intervals, and adequate rest. First graders begin to recognize that their behavior affects their health and safety. Some ways they demonstrate this are:

• dressing appropriately for the weather (knowing to wear mittens, gloves, hat, or scarf when it is cold outside);

• washing hands before snack or lunch times, and after using the bathroom;

• using tissues to wipe runny noses;

• identifying people who can help in emergency situations.

Second Grade

1 Shows understanding of how to maintain physical health and well-being.

The first step in keeping oneself healthy and safe is knowing what the body needs to function properly: regular toilet use and other personal hygiene, nutritious food at regular intervals, and adequate rest. Second graders should be able to recognize ways their behavior affects their health and safety. Some ways they demonstrate this include:

• washing hands before lunch and after going to the bathroom;

• covering their nose or mouth when sneezing and coughing;

• knowing and obeying fire drill rules;

• looking both ways before crossing the street.

Third Grade

1 Shows understanding of how to maintain physical health and well-being.

By third grade, children can understand what is needed to keep the body healthy and safe: nutritious food, adequate rest, and personal hygiene. They recognize how their behavior affects their own well-being. They demonstrate this by:

• using actions that help prevent germs from spreading (such as covering their nose or mouth when coughing and sneezing, and washing and drying hands before handling food);

• knowing and obeying fire drill rules;

• keeping their body and hair clean and neat;

• following traffic safety rules (such as crossing at corners, looking both ways, not running into the street to get a ball);

• identifying practices that might be dangerous to health (such as smoking, drinking, and using drugs).

Fourth Grade

1 Shows familiarity and knowledge of current issues related to health and safety.

Fourth graders have some basic understanding of the importance of maintaining good health habits and abiding by safety rules. Although many health and safety-related issues are beyond their control, they can ask questions and seek out information about a variety of these issues during the school day. Examples include:

• participating in group discussions that focus on a major health or safety issue (e.g., nutrition, first aid, drugs/alcohol, AIDS, personal safety);

• writing a response to a presentation related to personal well-being;

• presenting a report on how alcohol or drugs affect different organs or body systems;

• dramatizing how a biological system is affected by poor lifestyle choices (the effects of smoking on respiration and prenatal development).

Fifth Grade

1 Shows familiarity and knowledge of current issues related to health and safety.

By the time children are ten, they want to be considered independent enough to make decisions affecting their health and safety, and sometimes challenge adult decisions. They can be expected to talk, debate, question, research, and write about health and safety issues that indicate they have established a firm understanding of basic good habits and rules. Examples include:

• participating in group discussions that focus on major health or safety issues (for example, nutrition, first aid, drugs/alcohol, AIDS, personal safety);

• writing a personal response to a presentation about health or safety issues;

• presenting a report on a special area of interest that relates to health or safety;

• role playing in skits that dramatize the consequences of good or poor decision-making related to health and safety issues.

VII Physical Development

C Personal health and safety continued

Kindergarten	First Grade	Second Grade
2 Shows interest in health and safety issues.	**No equivalent performance indicator at this level.**	**No equivalent performance indicator at this level.**

Five year olds show awareness of many health and safety issues. At this age, children are most interested in these issues when they relate to their own experiences. Children show their awareness of these issues by:

• discussing traffic safety rules as they engage in dramatic play or build roads and cities out of blocks;

• talking with each other about the foods they eat during snack or lunch times;

• telling a friend not to run in front of the school bus or a car;

• discussing safety rules when on a class trip;

• discussing the roles of dentists and doctors in keeping people healthy;

• understanding why fire drills are important.

Third Grade

No equivalent performance indicator at this level.

Fourth Grade

No equivalent performance indicator at this level.

Fifth Grade

No equivalent performance indicator at this level.

VII Physical Development

C Personal health and safety continued

Kindergarten

No equivalent performance indicator at this level.

First Grade

No equivalent performance indicator at this level.

Second Grade

No equivalent performance indicator at this level.

Third Grade

No equivalent performance indicator at this level.

Fourth Grade

2 **Uses problem-solving methods and makes decisions that promote personal well-being.**

Nine year olds are presented with increasing responsibilities as they become more independent. Although they need opportunities to act responsibly, they continue to require limits that help them to feel safe. They still look primarily to family members for information and guidance even though they are beginning to identify with groups outside the family. Most nine year olds are extremely well-intentioned and want to be trusted to make healthy decisions. Examples include:

• participating in class discussions about drugs and alcohol (myths and facts, high-risk attributes, suggesting alternatives);

• recognizing outcomes related to specific decisions (writing graffiti on a wall will ruin the wall's appearance);

• taking responsibility for decisions and actions (following playground rules, or traffic laws when riding a bicycle in the street);

• offering or asking for help when needed (during a work period or out on the playground).

Fifth Grade

2 **Uses problem-solving methods and makes decisions that promote personal well-being.**

Ten year olds are starting to identify with influences outside the family. They often look to various groups (scouts, athletic groups, teachers, clubs, religious groups) beyond their families as resources to help them with their problem-solving and decision-making skills. They are more willing to listen to peers and others outside the family. Some examples include:

• offering help to others when needed (inviting a friend over who usually goes home to an empty house);

• recognizing outcomes related to specific decisions (smoking in the bathroom may result in a school suspension);

• taking responsibility for their decisions;

• refusing potentially dangerous invitations (leaving school grounds, fighting, climbing on the school's roof).

Resources

The following sources were of great help to us in preparing these materials:

Standards Setting Documents

American Association for the Advancement of Science (1993). *Project 2061: Benchmarks for Science Literacy.* New York: Oxford University Press.

Bredekamp, S. (Ed.), (1987). *Developmentally appropriate practice in early childhood programs serving children from birth through age 8.* Washington, DC: National Association for the Education of Young Children.

Center for the Study of Reading at The University of Illinois, The International Reading Association, The National Council of Teachers of English (1993). *Standards Project for English Language Arts: A Collection of Documents for the English Language Arts Profession.* Draft document.

Michigan State Board of Education (1992). *Early Childhood Standards of Quality, Pre-K-2.* Lansing, MI: Early Childhood Education, Parenting, and Comprehensive School Health Unit.

National Assessment Governing Board, U.S. Department of Education (1994). *Science Framework for the 1994 National Assessment of Educational Progress.* Washington, DC: Author.

National Center for History in the Schools (1993). *National History Standards Project (Progress Report and Sample Standards).* Los Angeles: UCLA/NEH.

National Council of Teachers of Mathematics (1992). *Curriculum and evaluation standards for school mathematics.* Reston, VA: Author.

National Council of Teachers of Mathematics (1993). *Curriculum and evaluation standards for school mathematics; addenda series, grades K–6.* Reston, VA: Author.

Curriculum Framework Materials

Ann Arbor Public Schools, Ann Arbor, MI—Grades 1–3 Mathematics

California State Department of Education — California Curriculum Frameworks for Mathematics and Science

Colorado Department of Education — Colorado Sample Outcomes and Proficiencies for Elementary, Middle, and High School Education

Maine Department of Education — Maine's Common Core of Learning

Michigan State Board of Education — Michigan Essential Goals and Objectives for Mathematics Education

Michigan State Board of Education — Michigan Essential Goals and Objectives for Social Studies Education

Michigan State Board of Education — Michigan Essential Goals and Objectives for Reading Education

Michigan State Board of Education — Michigan Essential Goals and Objectives for Writing

Minnesota Department of Education — Model Learner Outcomes for Early Childhood Education

North Carolina State Department of Education — North Carolina Standard Course of Study for Mathematics and Language Arts

Portland Public Schools, Portland, OR — Curriculum Framework for Science, Mathematics, and Social Studies for Grades K–3

South Carolina State Board of Education — South Carolina Mathematics Framework

Texas Education Agency — Texas Assessment of Academic Standards

The University of the State of New York — Social Studies Programs 4 & 5

Vermont State Department of Education — A Guide to Curriculum Development

Vermont State Department of Education — The Vermont Common Core of Learning, Education for the 21st Century

Vermont State Department of Education — Vermont Mathematics Portfolio Project

Vermont State Department of Education — Vermont Assessment: The Pilot Year

Virginia Department of Education — Virginia Standards of Learning Objectives for Language Arts, Mathematics, and Science

The Washington State Guidelines for K–12 Social Studies Education

Wellesley Public Schools, Wellesley, MA — Science Curriculum

Additional Resources

Ames, L.B., & Ilg, F.L. (1979). *Your five year old.* New Haven, CT: Gesell Institute of Human Development.

Anthony, R.J., Johnson, T.D., Mickelson, N.I., & Preece, A. (1991). *Evaluating literacy.* Portsmouth, NH: Heinemann Educational Books, Inc.

Baker, A., & Baker, J. (1990). *Mathematics in process.* Portsmouth, NH: Heinemann Educational Books, Inc.

Barrs, M., Ellis, S., Hester, H., & Thomas, A. (1989). *The Primary Language Record: Handbook for teachers.* Potsmouth, NY: Heinemann Educational Books, Inc.

Biber, B. (1942). *Life and ways of the seven to eight year old.* New York: Basic Books.

Biber, B. (1989). *Early education and psychological development.* New Haven, CT: Yale University Press.

Resources continued

Burns, M. (1992). *About teaching mathematics.* Sausalito, CA: Marilyn Burns Education Associates.

Calkins, L.M. (1986). *The art of teaching writing.* Portsmouth, NH: Heinemann Educational Books, Inc.

Charney, R. (1992). *Teaching children to care.* Greenfield, MA: Northeast Foundation for Children.

Cohen, D. (1973). *The learning child.* New York: Vintage Books.

Dodge, D.T. & Colker, L.J. (1992). *The Creative Curriculum for Early Childhood* (3rd ed.). Washington, D.C.: Teaching Strategies, Inc.

Doris, E. (1991). *Doing what scientists do: Children learn to investigate their world.* Portsmouth, NH: Heinemann Educational Books, Inc.

Gardner, H. (1973). *The arts and human development.* New York: John Wiley & Sons.

Gentry, J.R., & Gillet, J.W. (1993). *Teaching kids to spell.* Portsmouth, NH: Heinemann Educational Books, Inc.

Hartley, F., & Goldenson, M. (1952). *Understanding children's play.* New York: Columbia University Press.

Holdaway, D. (1980). *Independence in reading.* Gosford, NSW: Ashton Scholastic Press.

Hyde, A.A., & Hyde, P.R. (1991). *Mathwise.* Portsmouth, NH: Heinemann Educational Books, Inc.

Kephart, C. (1971). *The slow learner in the classroom.* Columbus, OH: Charles E. Merrill Publishing Co.

Konner, M. (1991). *Childhood: A Multicultural View.* Boston, MA: Little, Brown & Company.

Lane County Mathematics Project. (1983). *Problem solving in mathematics.* Palo Alto, CA: Dale Seymour Publications.

MacMillan/McGraw Hill (1993). *Performance Assessment Handbook.* Guide for Reading/Language Arts Teachers. Grades 1, 2, 3. New York: author.

Miller, K. (1985). *Ages and stages.* Telshare Publishing Company.

Mills, H. & Clyde, J.A. (1990). *Portraits of whole language classrooms.* Portsmouth, NH: Heinemann Educational Books, Inc.

Minuchin, P.P. (1977). *The middle years of childhood.* Monterey, CA: Brooks/Cole Publishing Company.

Mitchell, A. & David, J. (Eds.) (1992). *Explorations with young children: A curriculum guide from The Bank Street College of Education.* Mt. Ranier, MD: Gryphon House.

Mitchell, L.S. (1991). *Young geographers.* New York: Bank Street College of Education.

National Council of Teachers of Mathematics. (1991). *Mathematics assessment: myths, models, good questions and practical suggestions.* Reston, VA: Jean Kerr Stenmark.

Neugebauer, B. (Ed.) (1992). *Alike and different: Exploring our humanity with young children.* Washington, DC: National Association for the Education of Young Children.

Osborne, R. & Freyberg, P. (1985). *Learning in science.* Portsmouth, NH: Heinemann Educational Books, Inc.

Patterson, J. (1977). Criterion model for preschool curriculum. In S. Provence, A. Naylor, & J. Patterson (Eds.), *The challenge of day care.* New Haven, CT: Yale University Press.

Payne, J. (1975). *Mathematics learning in early childhood.* Reston, VA: National Council of Teachers of Mathematics.

Peterson, R., & Felton-Collins, V. (1986). *The Piaget handbook for teachers and parents.* New York: Teachers College Press.

Resources continued

Pitcher, E.G., Lasher, M.G., Feinburg, S., & Hammond, N.C. (1966). *Helping young children learn.* Columbus. OH: Charles E. Merrill Publishing Co.

Renner, J. & Marek, E. (1988). *The learning cycle and elementary school science teaching.* Portsmouth, NH: Heinemann Educational Books, Inc.

Rhodes, L.K., & Shanklin, N. (1993). *Windows into literacy.* Portsmouth, NH: Heinemann Educational Books, Inc.

Rogers, C.S., & Sawters, J.K. (1988). *Play in the lives of children.* Washington, DC: NAEYC.

Routman, R. (1988). *Transitions: From literature to literacy.* Portsmouth, NH: Heinemann Educational Books, Inc.

Routman, R. (1991). *Invitations: Changing as teachers and learners, K–12.* Toronto: Irwin Publishing Company.

Science 5/13 Series. (1973). London: Macdonald Educational.

Singer, D.S., & Ryenson, T.A. (1978). *A Piaget primer: How a child thinks.* New York: Plume and Meridian Books.

Stenmark, J.K., Thompson, V., & Cossey, R. (1986). *Family math.* Berkeley, CA: University of California.

Taba, H., Durkin, M., Fraenkel, J., & McNaughton, A. (1971). *A teacher's handbook to elementary social studies.* Addison-Wesley Publishing Company.

Weaver, C. (1990). *Understanding whole language: From principles to practice.* Portsmouth, NH: Heinemann Educational Books, Inc.

Wood, C. (1994). *Yardsticks: Children in the Classroom Ages 4–12.* Greenfield, MA: Northeast Foundation for Children.

Acknowledgements

This work was supported in part by a grant from the John D. and Catherine T. MacArthur Foundation awarded to Samuel J. Meisels. It was also assisted by support from the Brattleboro (VT) Follow Through Program and other sources.

In particular, we wish to thank the following individuals for their valuable suggestions and feedback:

From Brattleboro (VT) Public Schools: Jean Albee, Mary Alice and Peter Amidon, Pam Becker, Jim Bedard, John Bentley, Patricia Berger, Cathy Crafts-Allen, Michelle Cross, Kathy Ernst, Margerie Guthrie, Deborah Hall, Jennifer Irion, Judie Jerald, Linda Jewett-Bell, Janis Kiehle, Polly Kurty, Lucille Messina, Donna Natowich, Flo Nestor, Charlotte Stetson, Anthony Speranza, Katey Tobey, and Linn Wilson; From Bank Street College of Education (NYC): Joan Cenedella, Judith Gold, and Elizabeth Servidio; From Gilman School, Baltimore (MD): Wickes MacColl; From Park School, Baltimore (MD): Sharon Pula; From Wellesley (MA) Public Schools: Laura Thorpe Katz; From District of Columbia Public Schools: Austine Fowler, Martha Hansen, and Parker Anderson; From Pittsburgh (PA) Public Schools: Diane Briars and Joanne Eresh; From Newfane (VT) Public Schools: David Parker; From Putney (VT) Public Schools: Henny Walsh; From Health Education Resource Center, Vermont Department of Education: JoEllen Falk.

Teachers and staff from the following districts have played an ongoing role in the development of Work Sampling: Willow Run (MI) Community Schools and Massachusetts Project Impact, including the districts of Agawam, Boston, Cambridge, Lynn, Lynn Economic Opportunity Head Start, Old Rochester, Pioneer Valley, and Somerset.

Teachers from the folowing school districts were instrumental in the early development of Work Sampling: Dexter (MI) Public Schools, Davison (MI) Public Schools, Flint (MI) Public Schools,

Acknowledgements continued

Northview (MI) Public Schools, and Fort Worth (TX) Independent School District.

Grateful acknowledgement is made to our colleague Aviva Dorfman, who reviewed every element of the Guidelines and who contributed substantially to them in many ways. In addition, we are extremely grateful to Joni Block of the Massachusetts Department of Education, Diane Trister Dodge of Teaching Strategies, Inc., Donna Bickel of the Pittsburgh Public Schools, and our Work Sampling colleagues who contributed to this effort, particularly Regena Fails and Sylvia Jones. Dorothy Steele made major contributions to the original formulation of the Work Sampling System. Others without whom this work could not have taken place include June Patterson, Toni Bickart, Sally Provence, Irving Marsden, and Thomas Trenchard. Sue Kelley, Jan Blomberg, Sally Atkins-Burnett, Pat McMahon, and Kris Kasperski of the University of Michigan assisted the project in countless ways. Finally, we are indebted to Tiff Crutchfield of Mode Design whose remarkable assistance in design, layout, and production has resulted in both the attractive appearance and systemic integrity of the Work Sampling materials.

Judy Jablon
Lauren Ashley
Dot Marsden
Sam Meisels
Margo Dichtelmiller